Make Me Smile

Artwork by Autumn Hope Anderson
Between age 5 and 6
2015-2016

Make Me Smile
by Autumn Hope Anderson
August 2016

Published by:

Life Application Ministries Publishing (LAMP)

P.O. Box 165
Mt. Aukum, CA 95656

Printer: createspace.com

Introduction

Autumn Hope Anderson is a very creative and wonderful little girl. At the age of five she began watching Youtube with her older sister and studied every move, every line, every bit of the artist's work. She then decided to try it herself. Much to everyone's surprise, including her own, she has created hundreds of pictures and designs.

We often would discuss who she received this wonderful gift from, after all, her grandmother, her grandfather and many others in the family displayed such skills as well. But, it was determined that she got it from her Father in Heaven, the Lord God who created her and gave her this gift of which we give Him all the glory.

It is our hope that you enjoy her drawings and see her heart behind each picture. It's amazing that such a young girl can draw with such depth and passion. Only the Lord knows where this will take her, but by encouraging her to continue, it is expected that she will go far. Her artwork can make one smile, thus the title of the book -

Make Me Smile

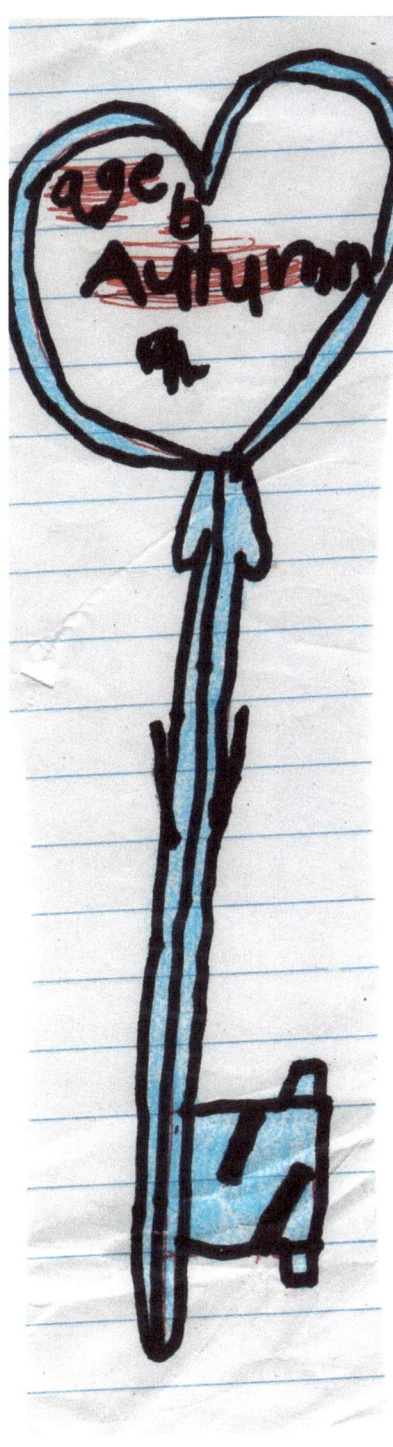

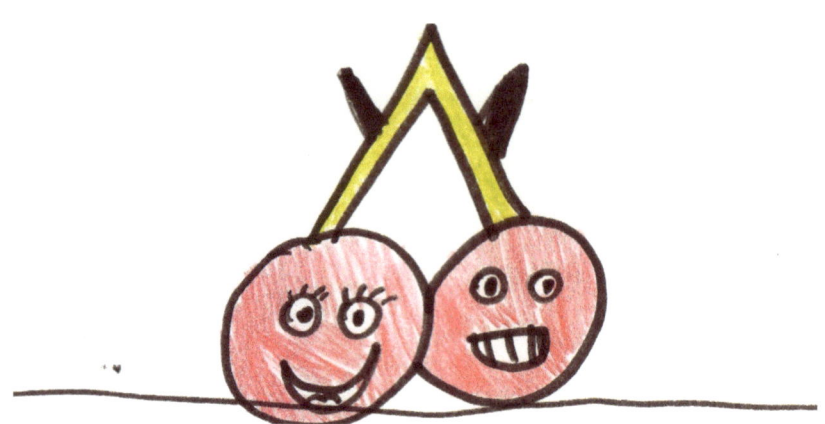

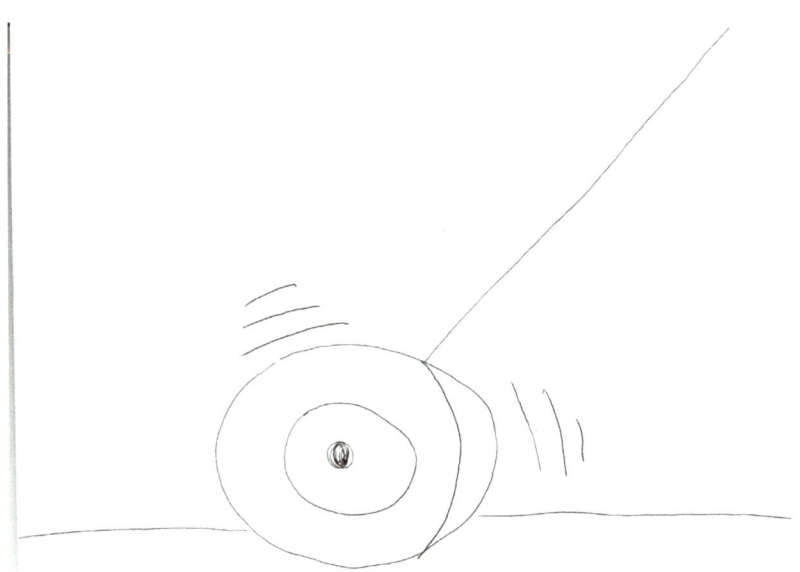

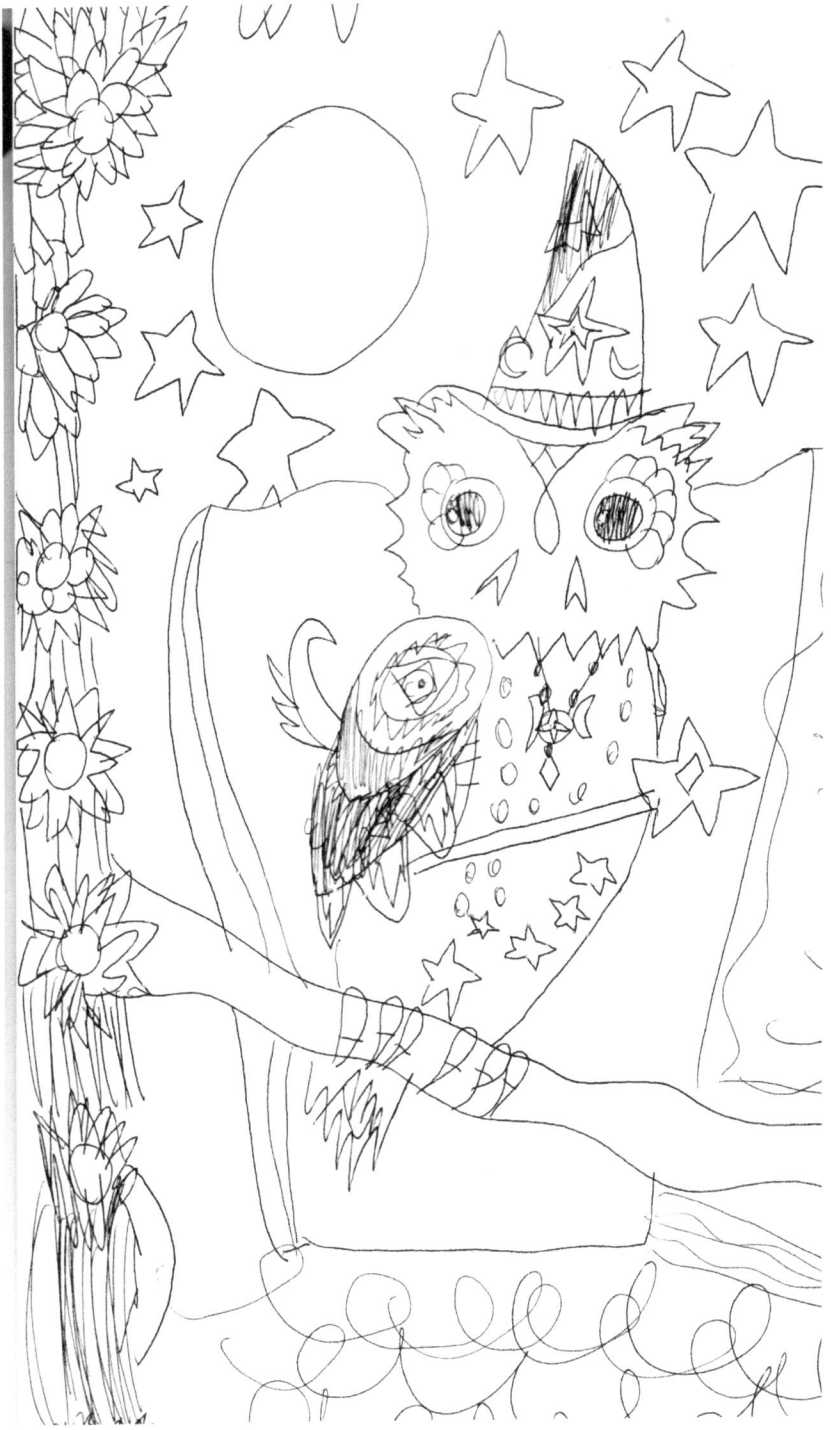

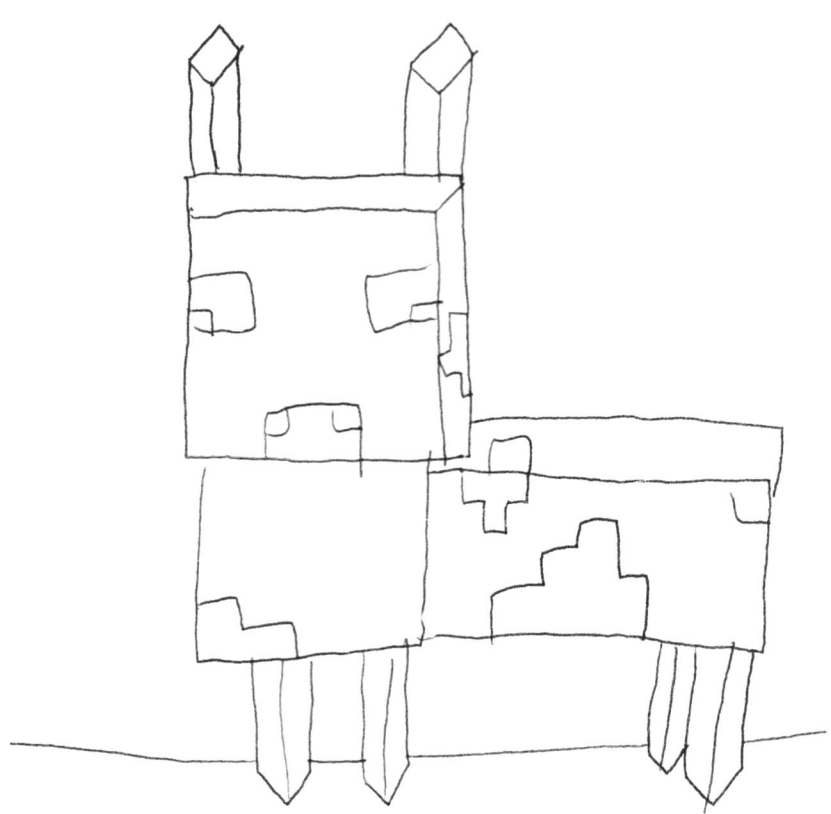

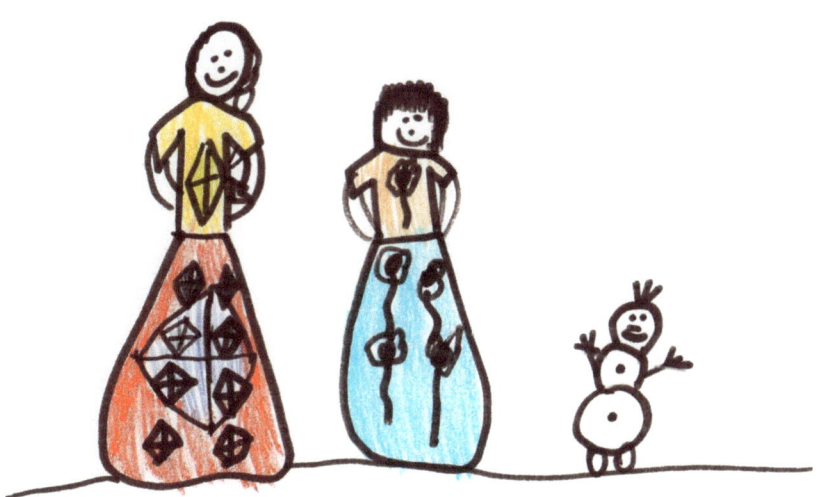

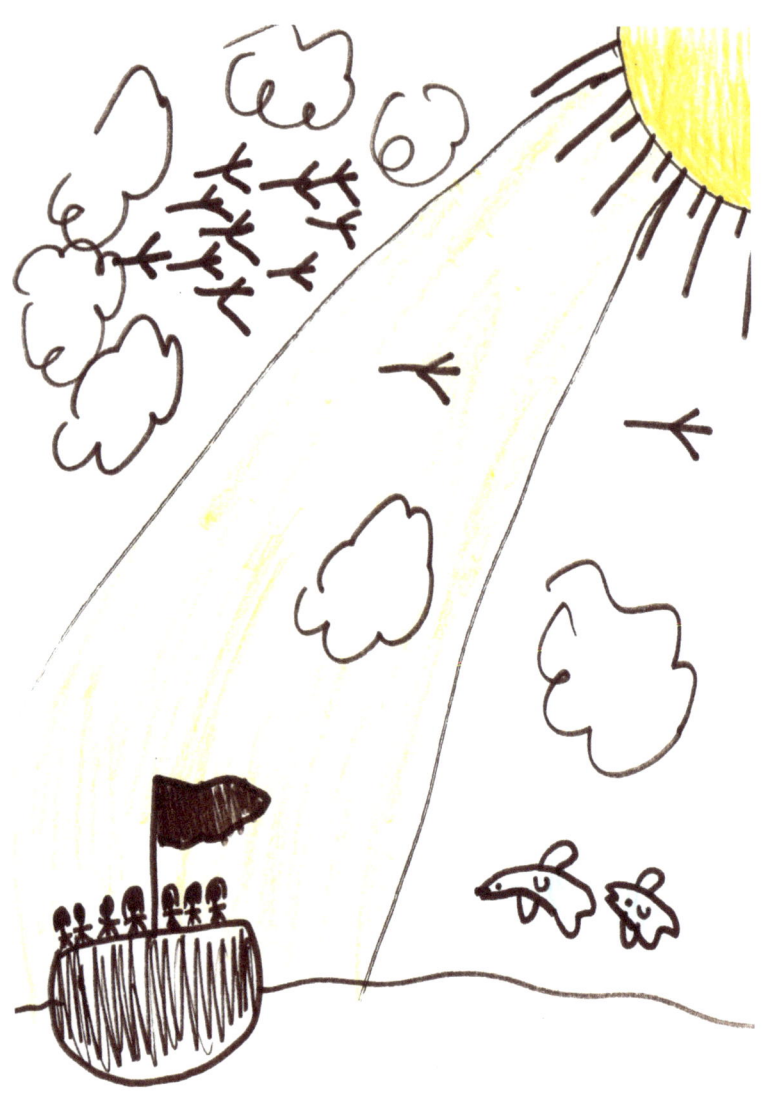

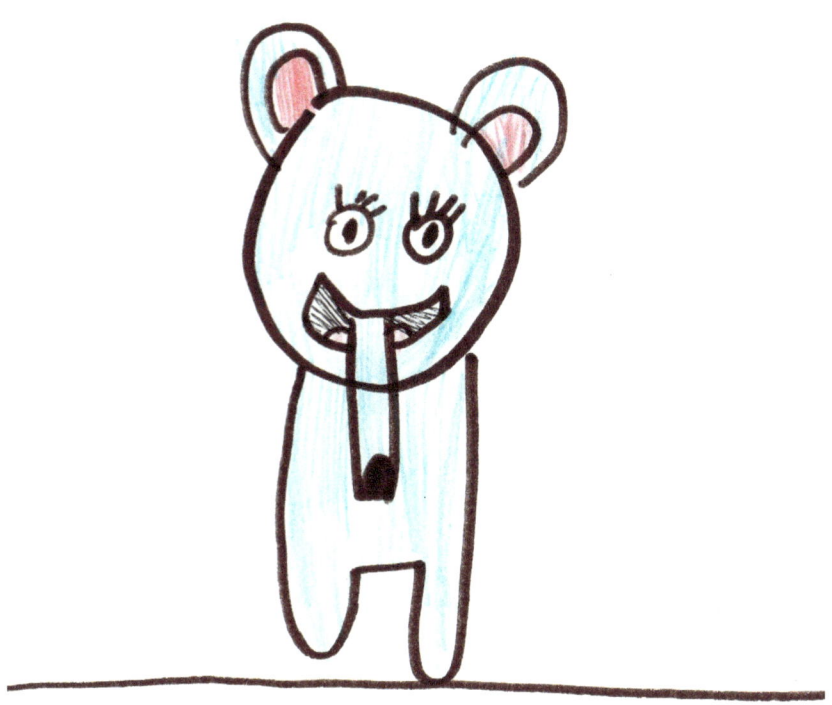

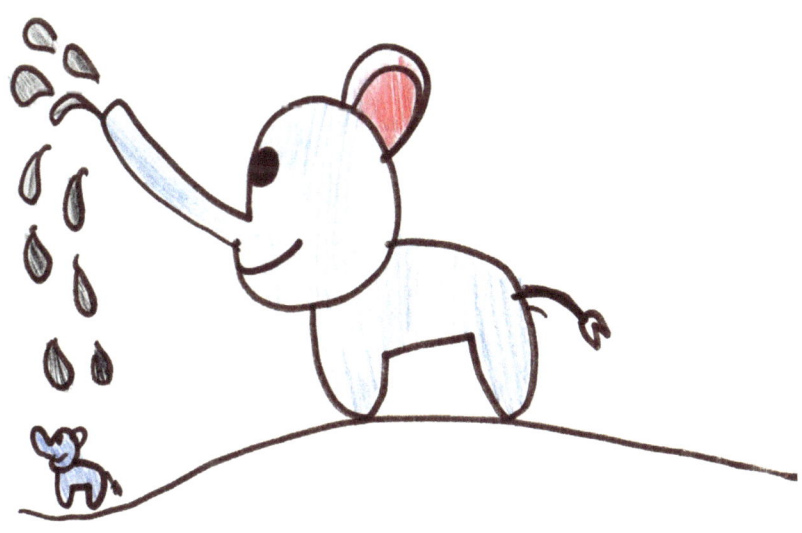

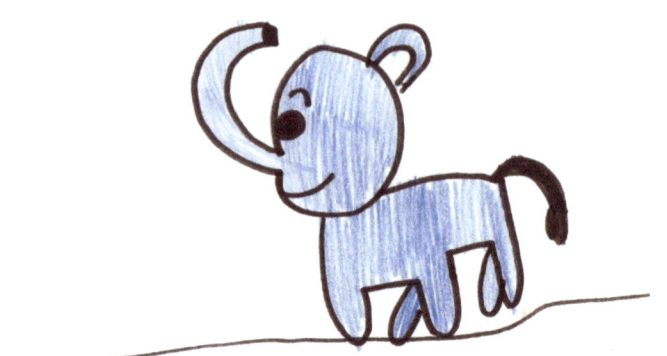

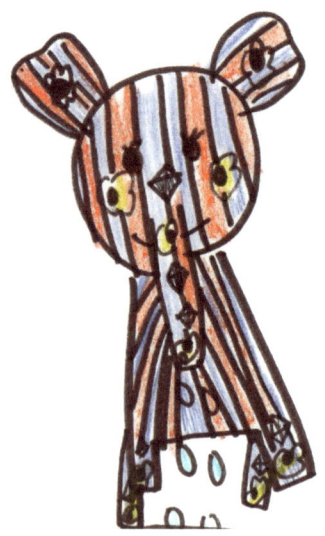

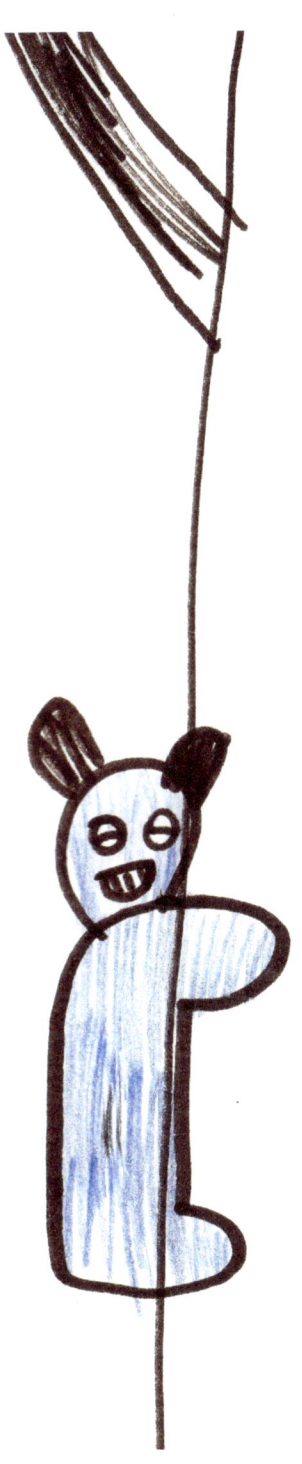

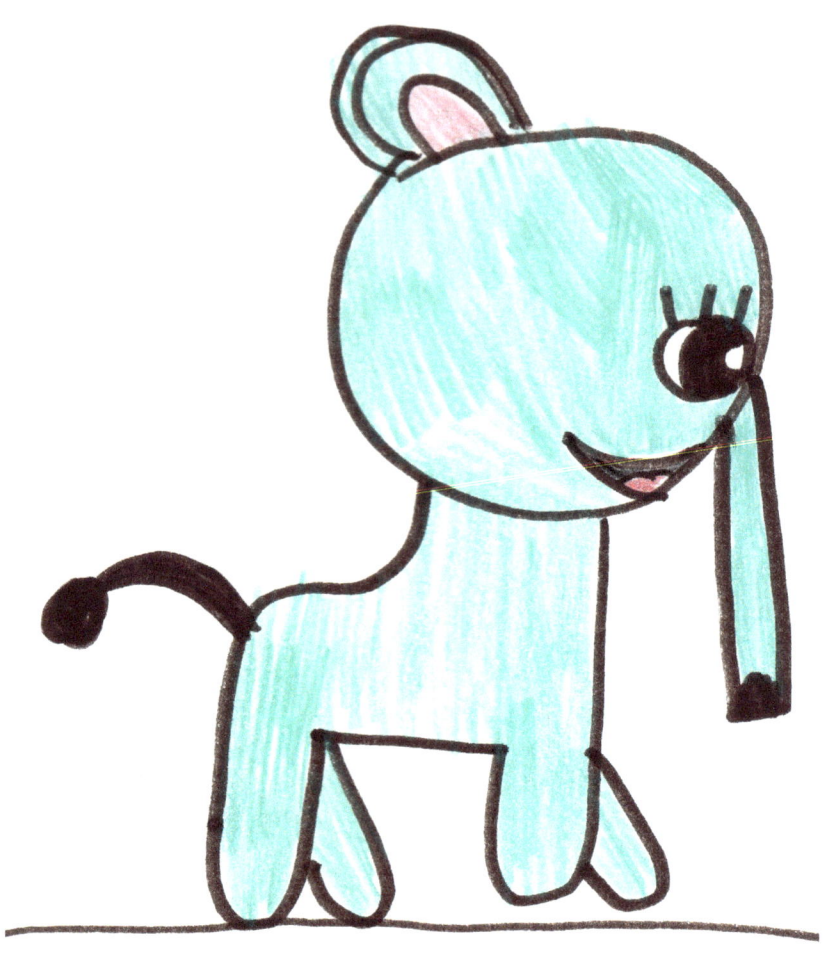

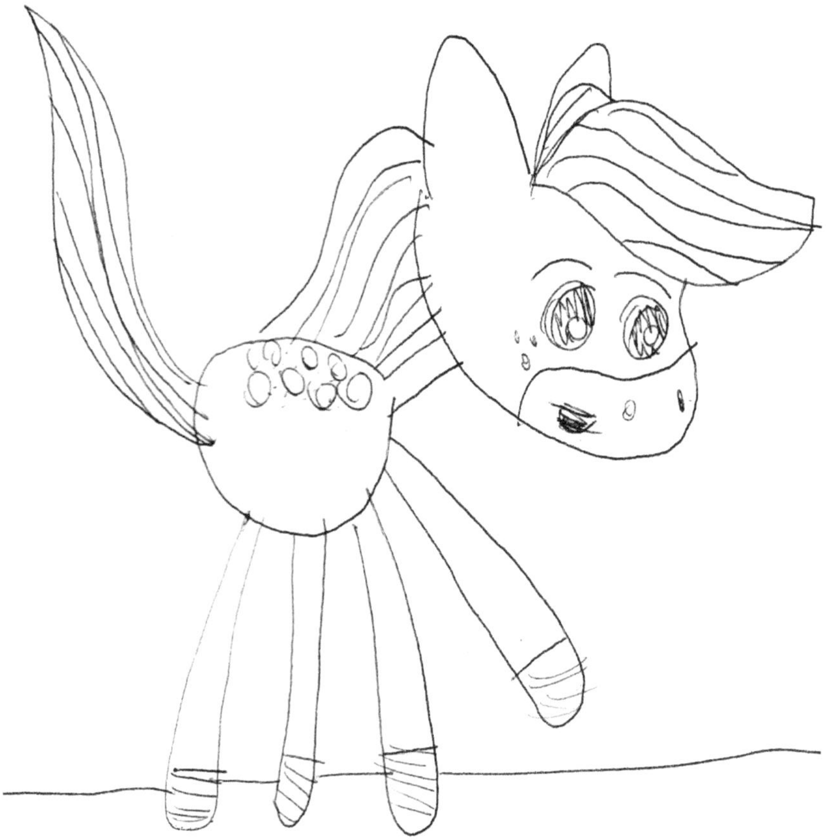

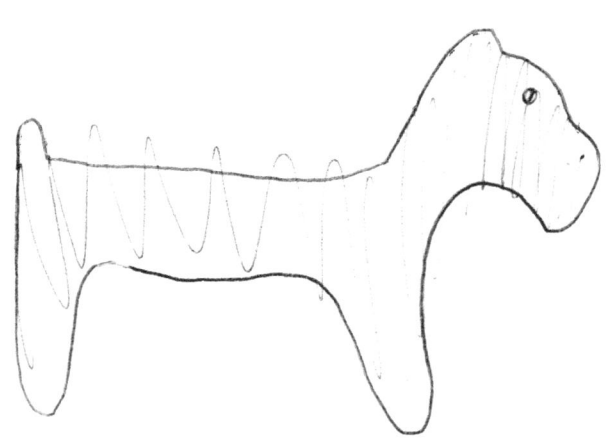

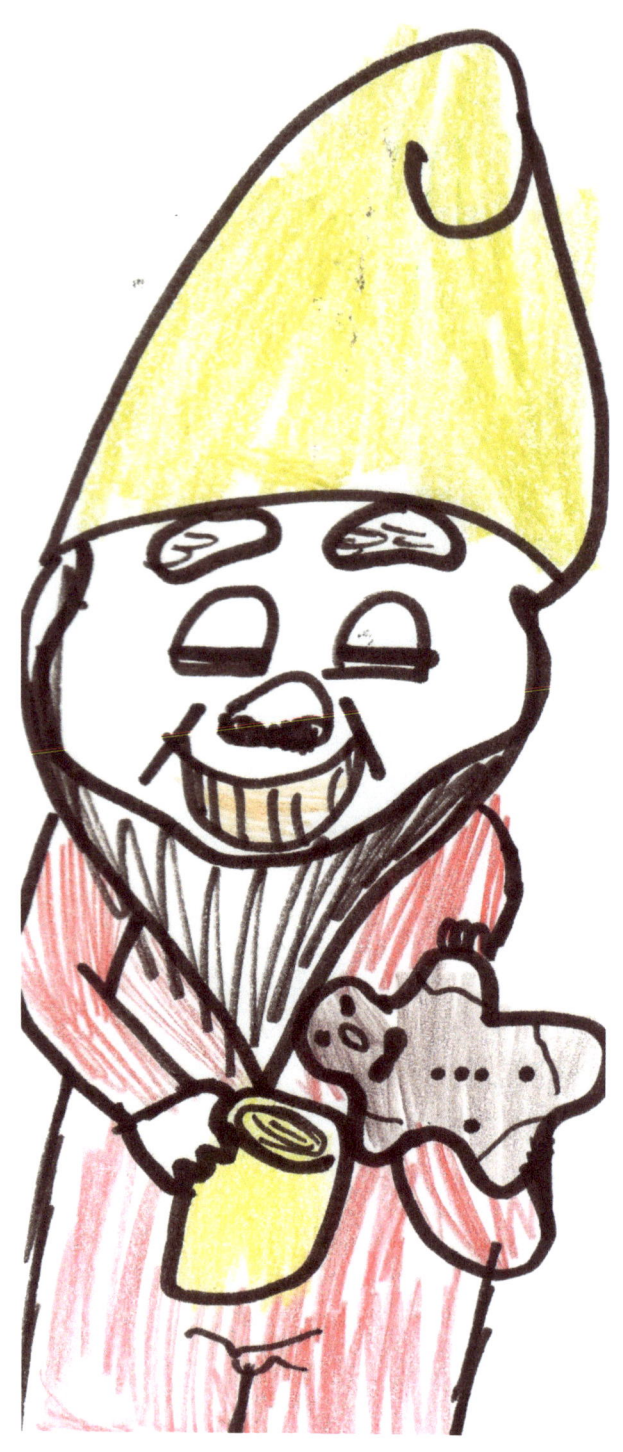

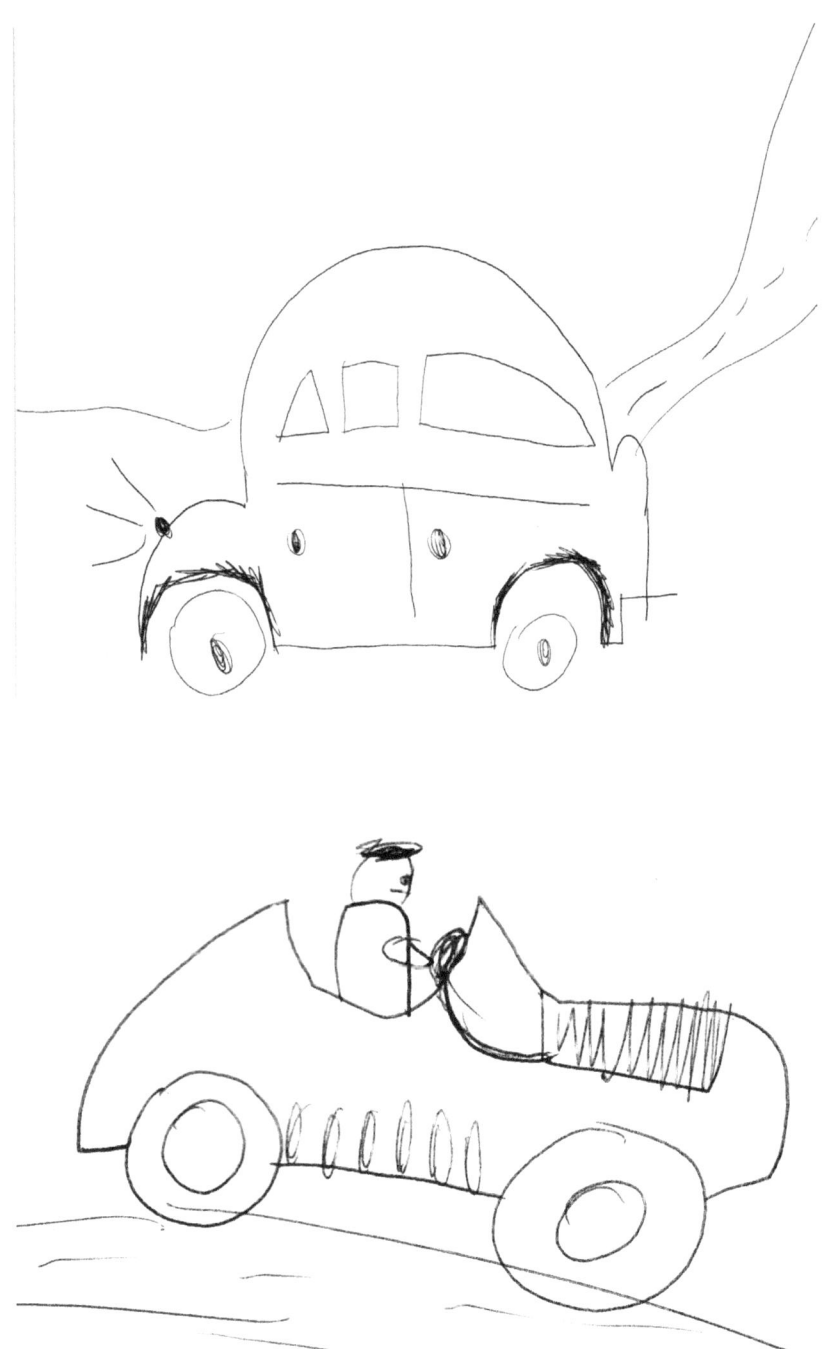

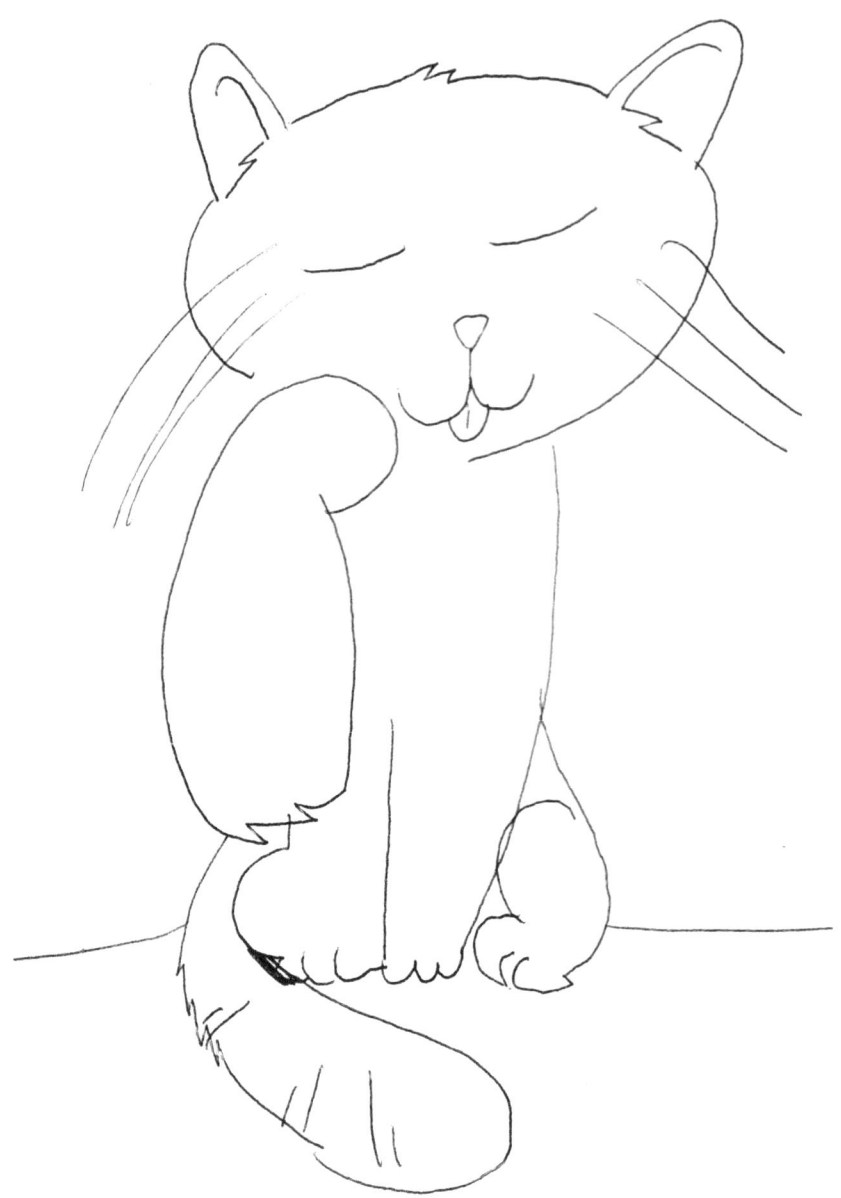

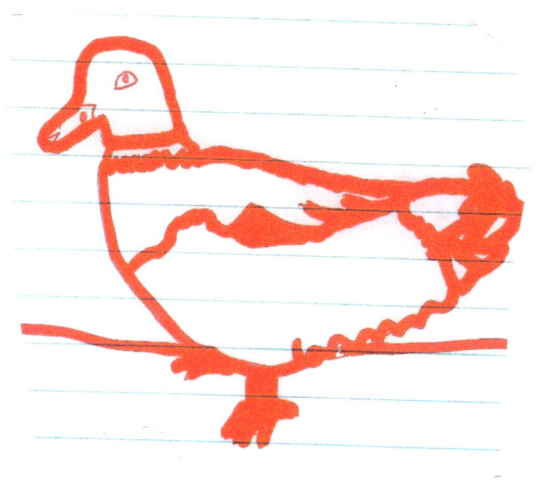

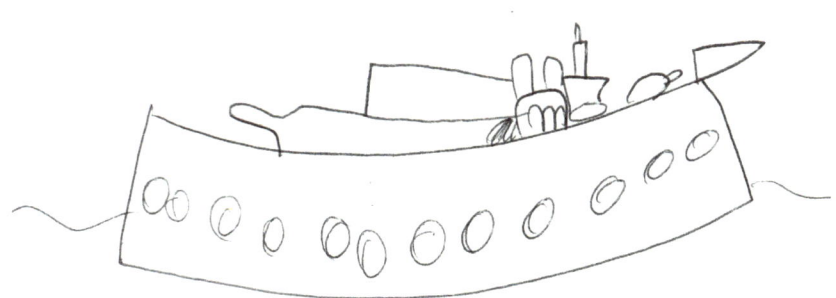

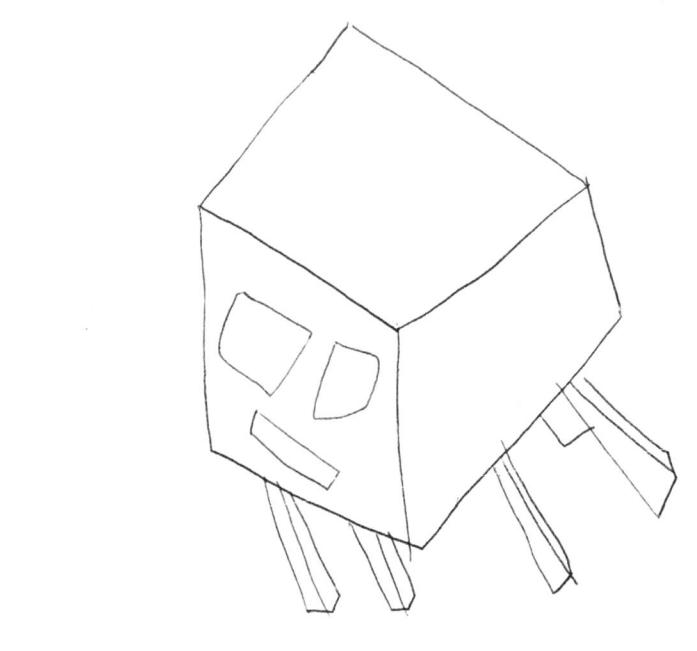

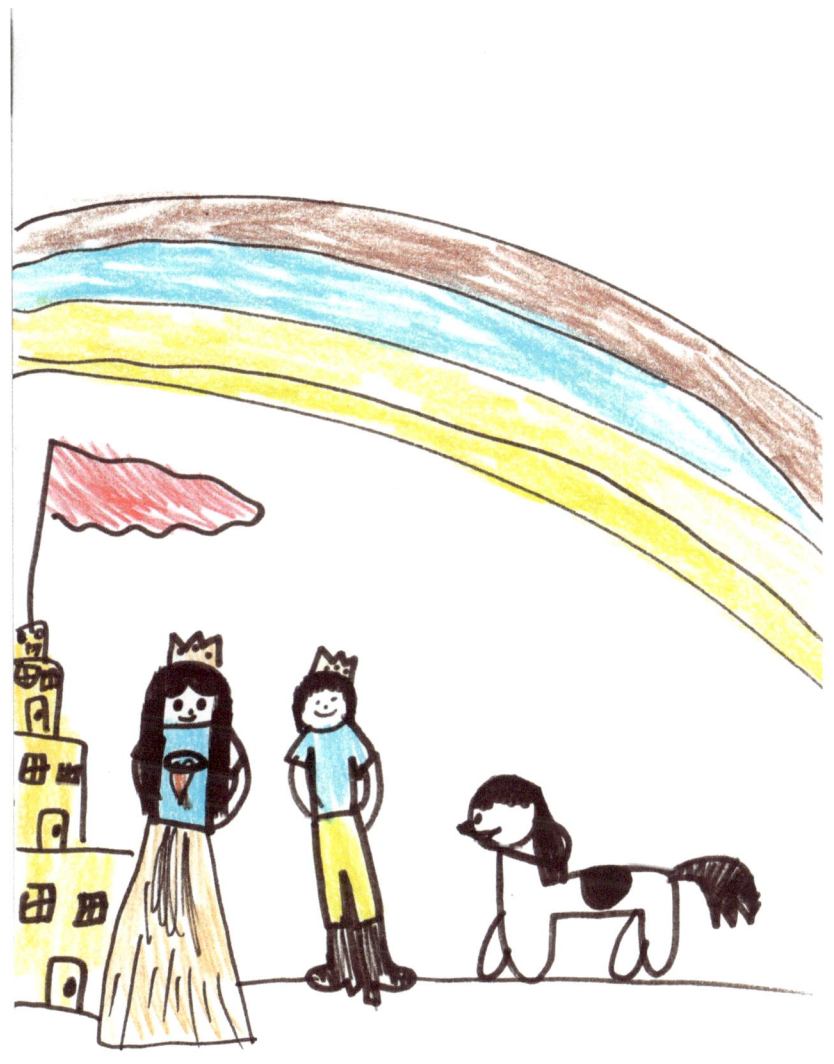

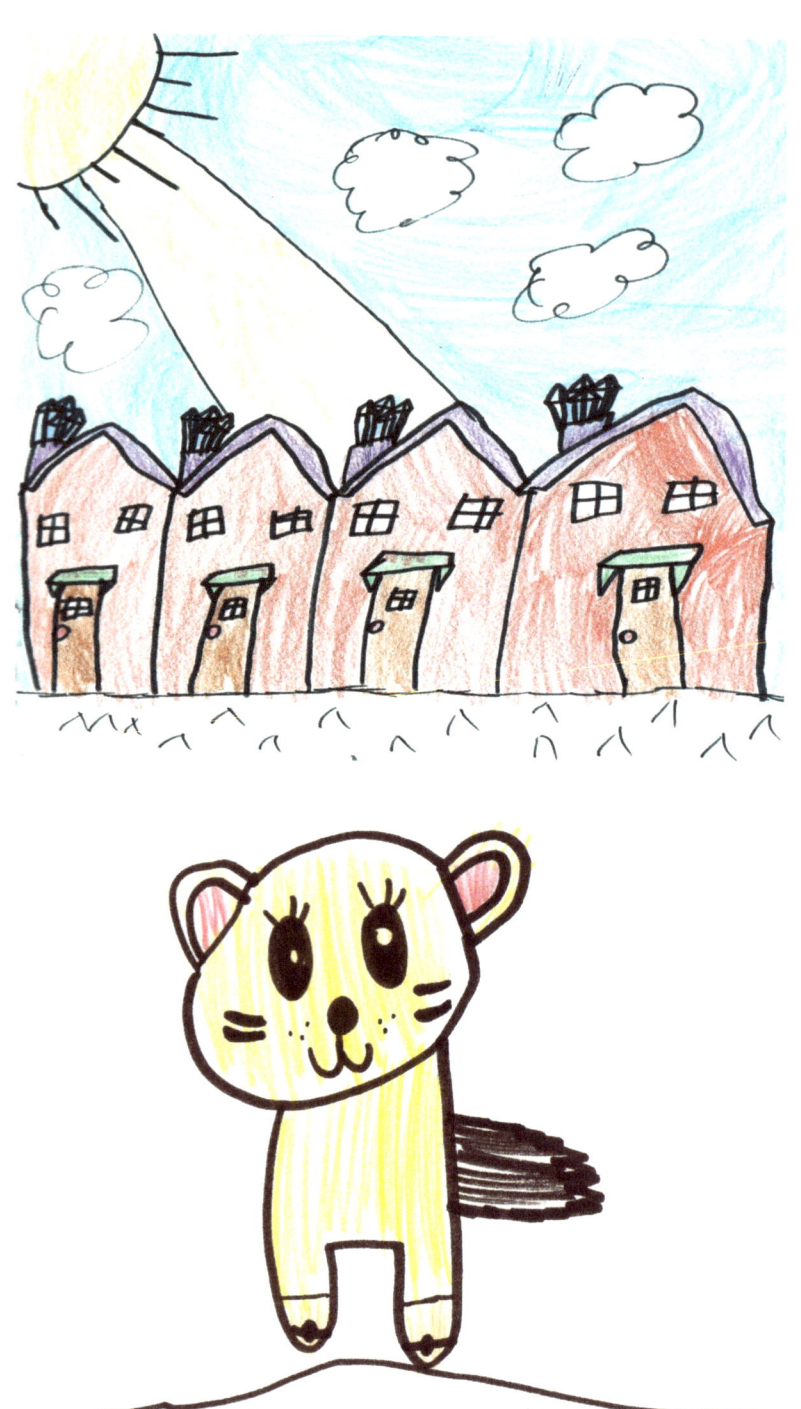

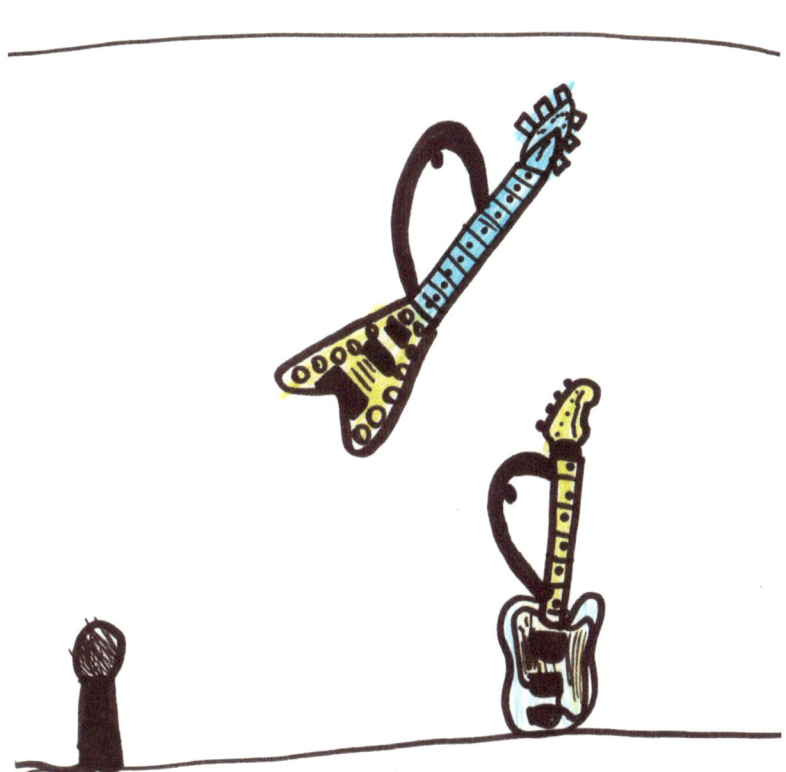

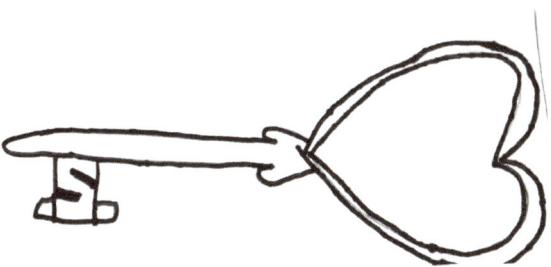

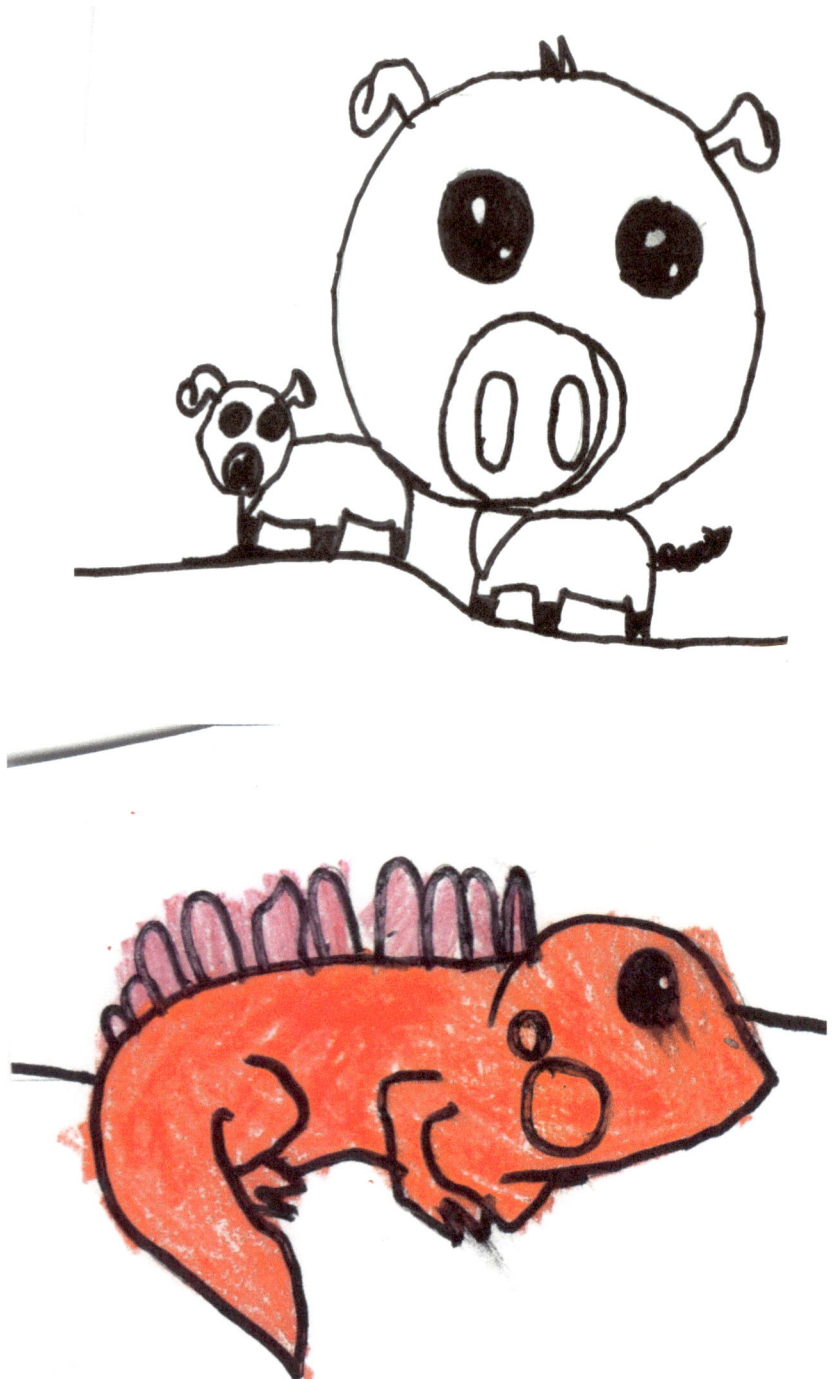

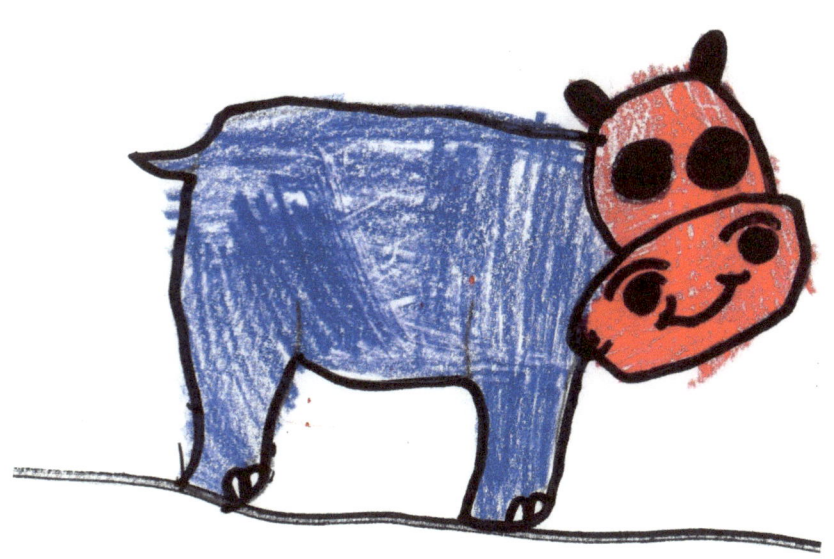

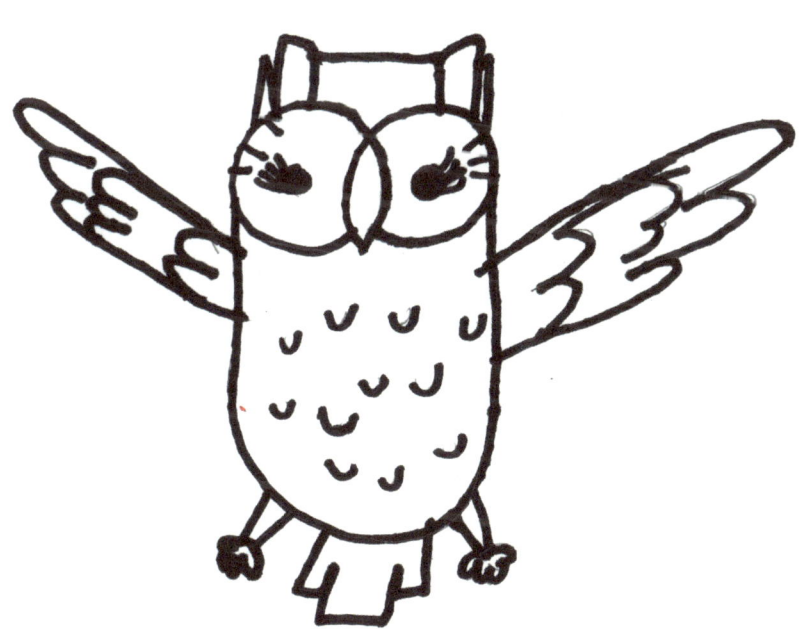

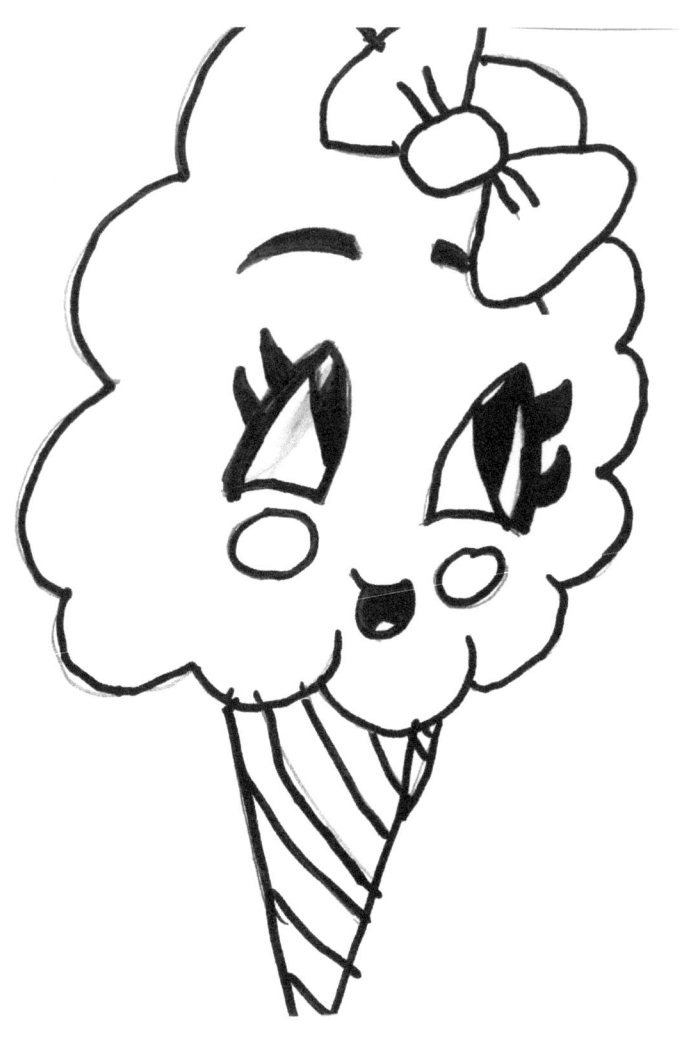

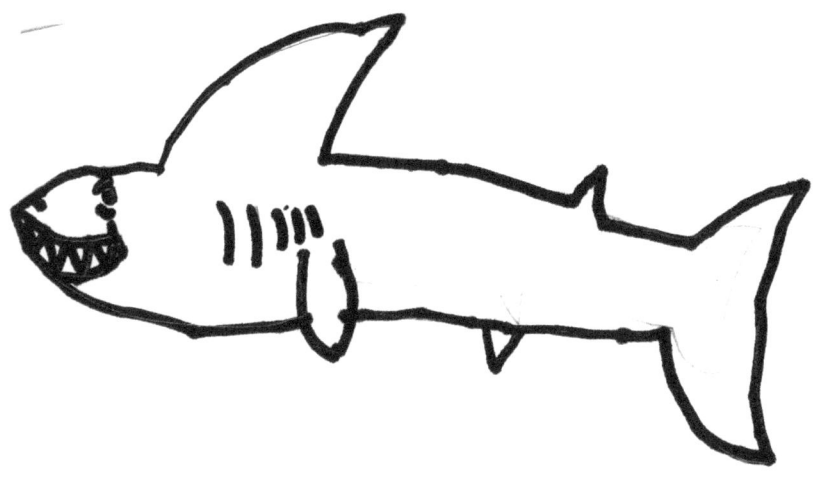

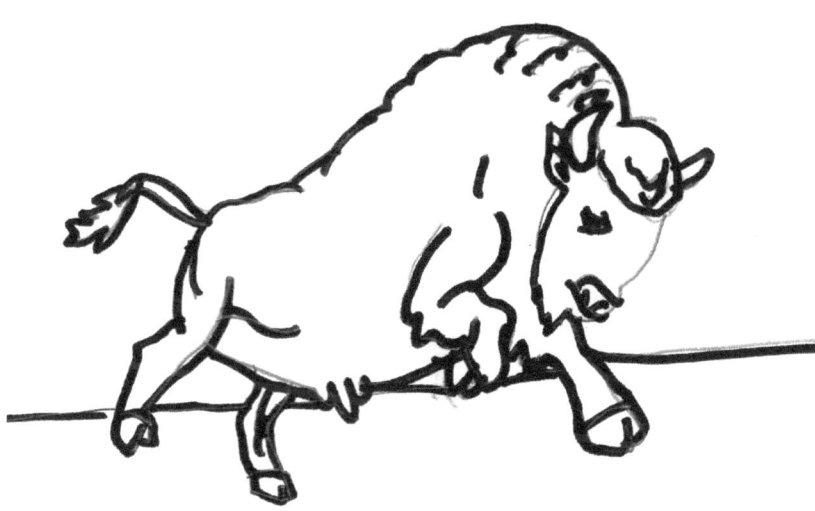

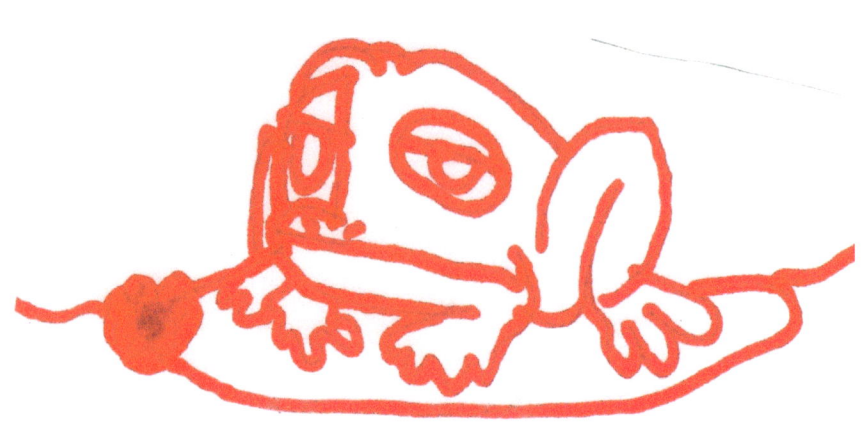

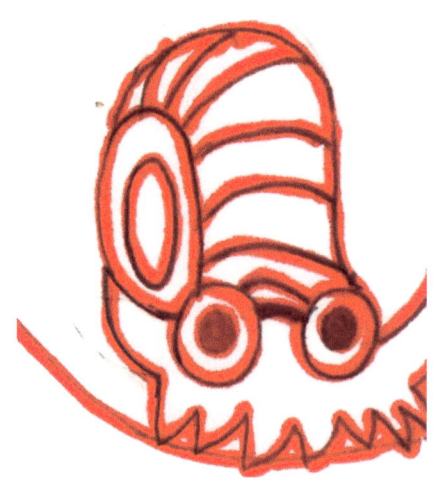

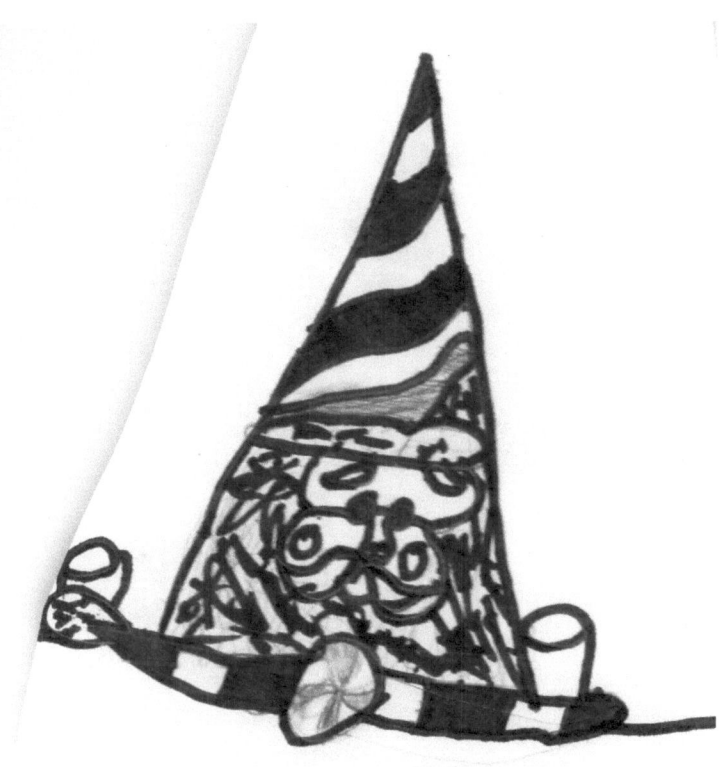

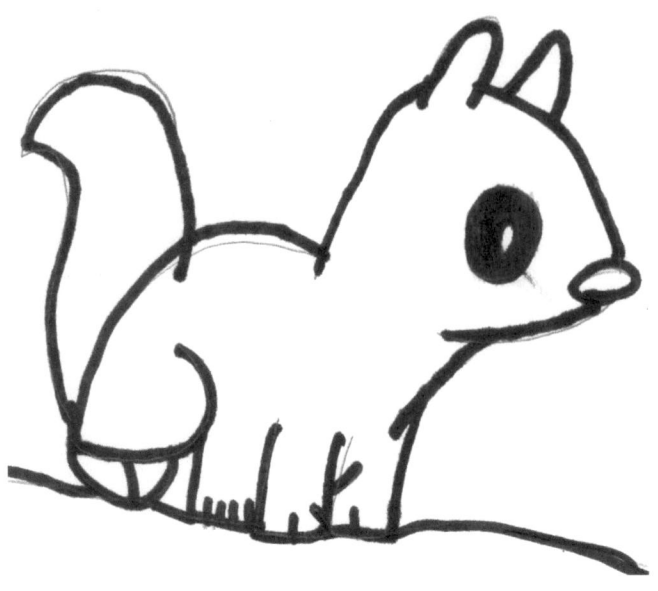

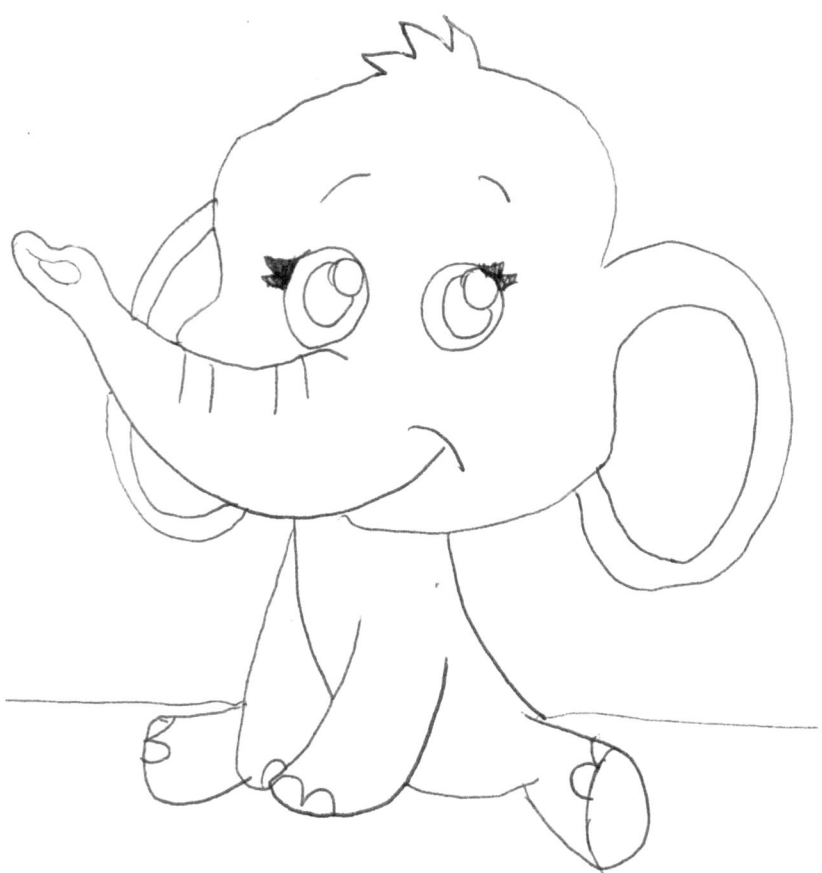

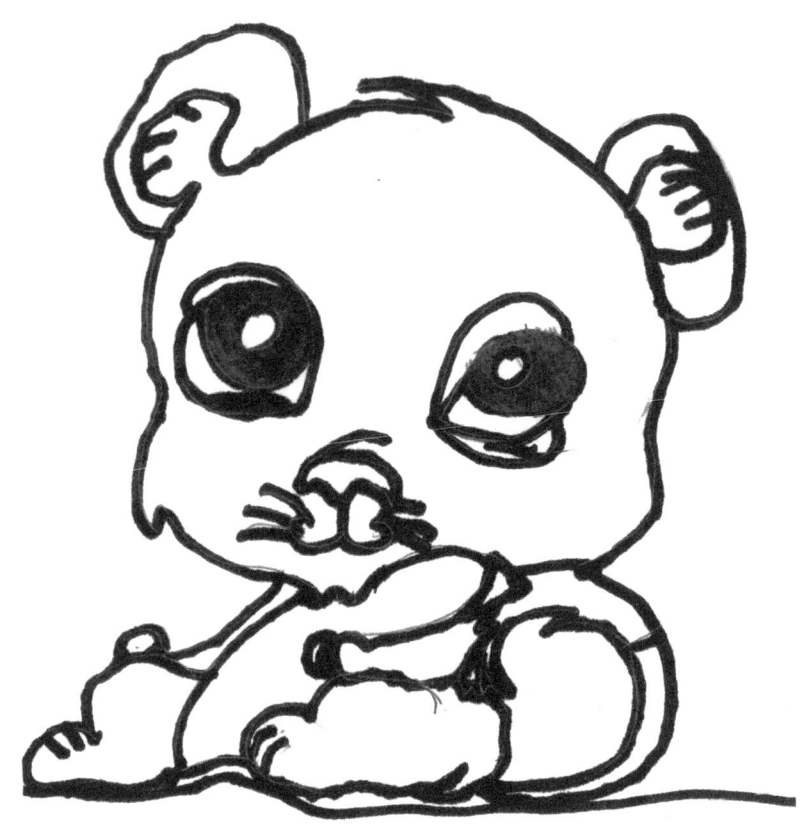

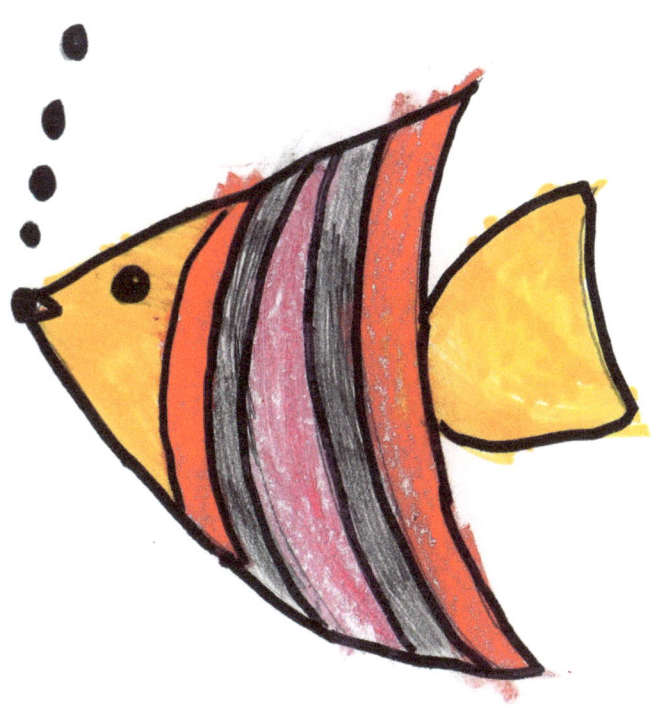

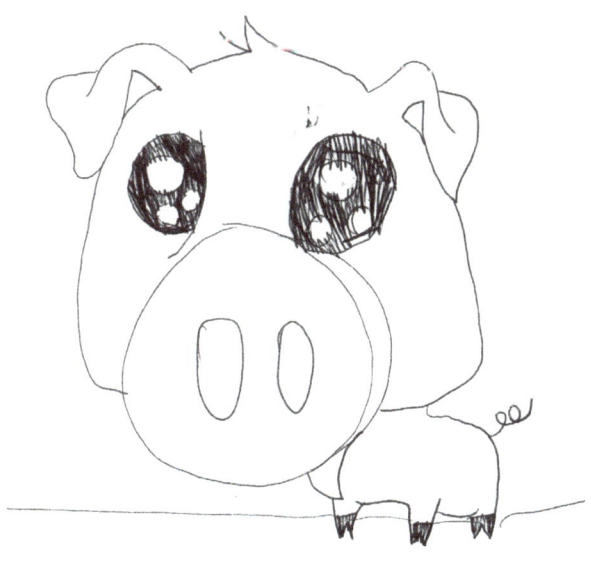

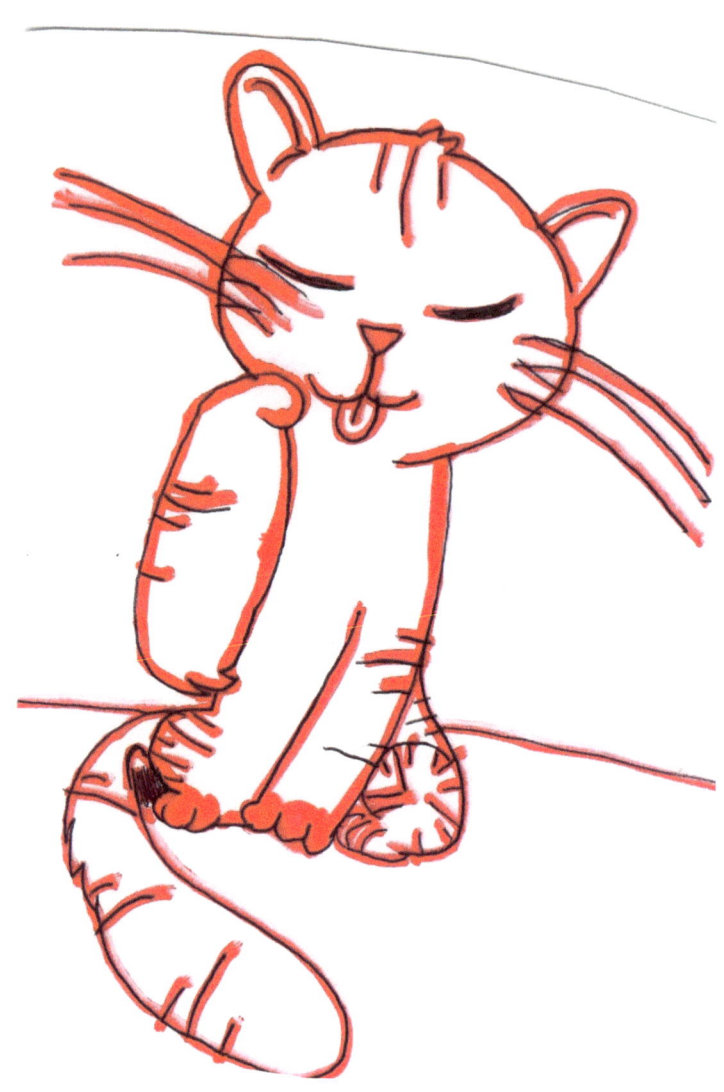

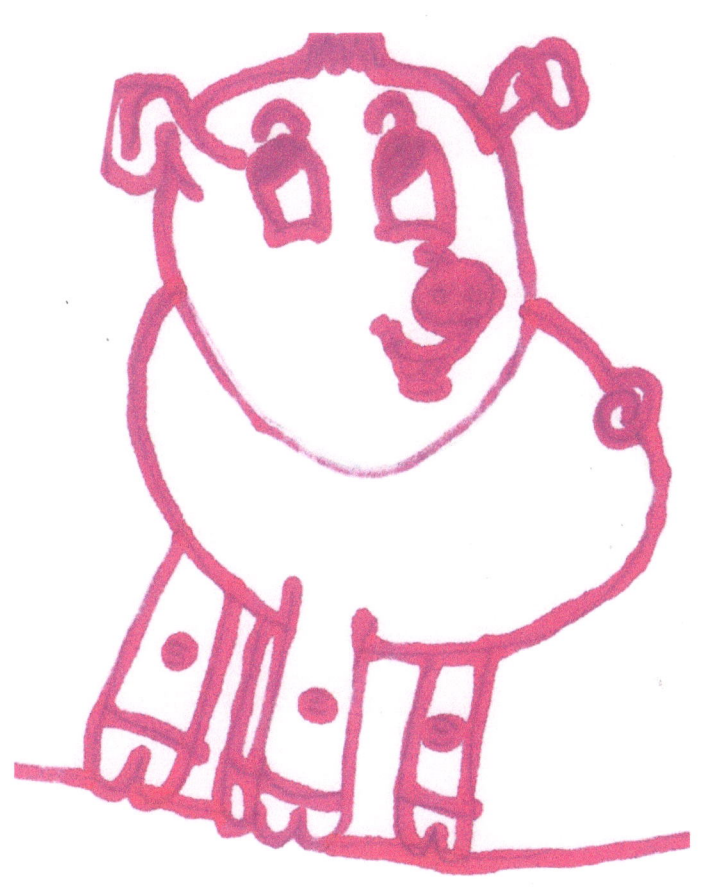

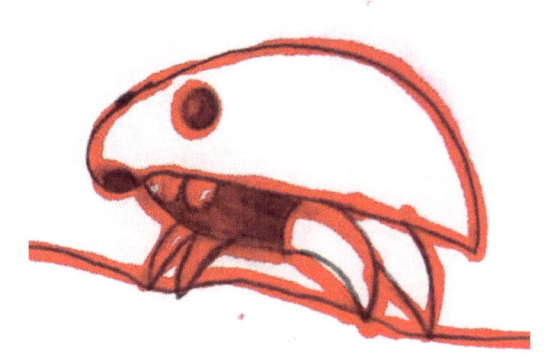

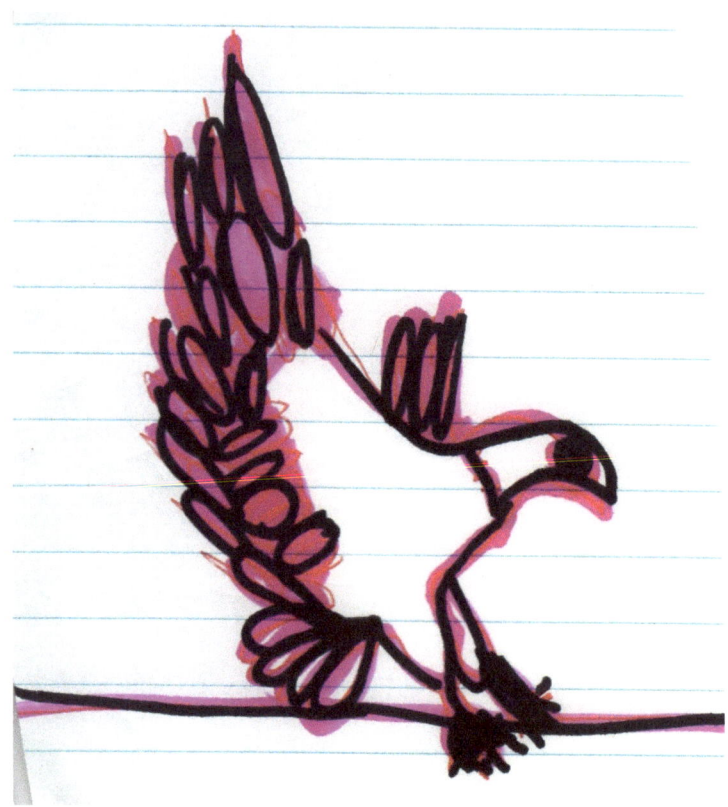

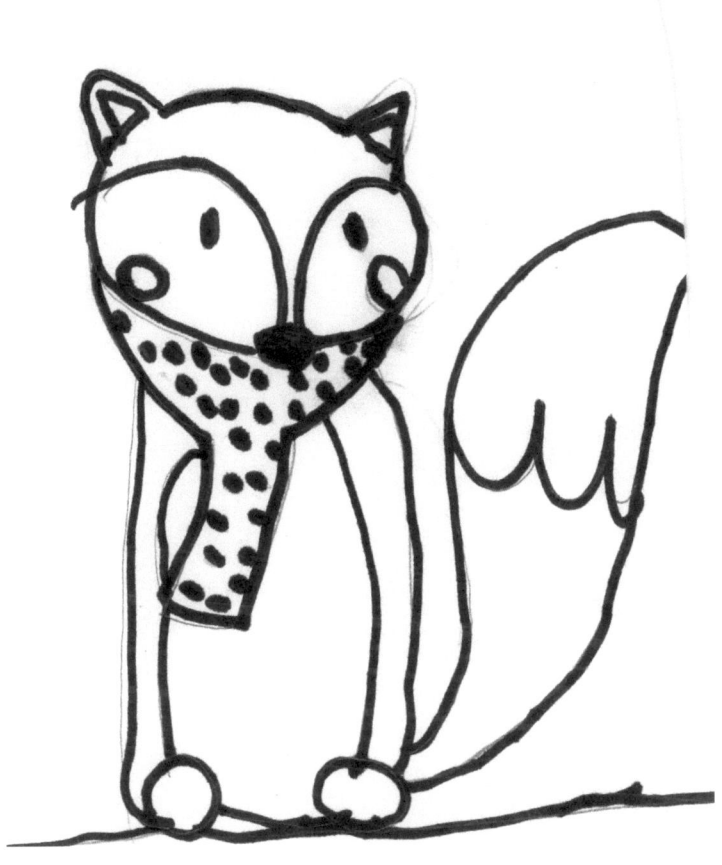

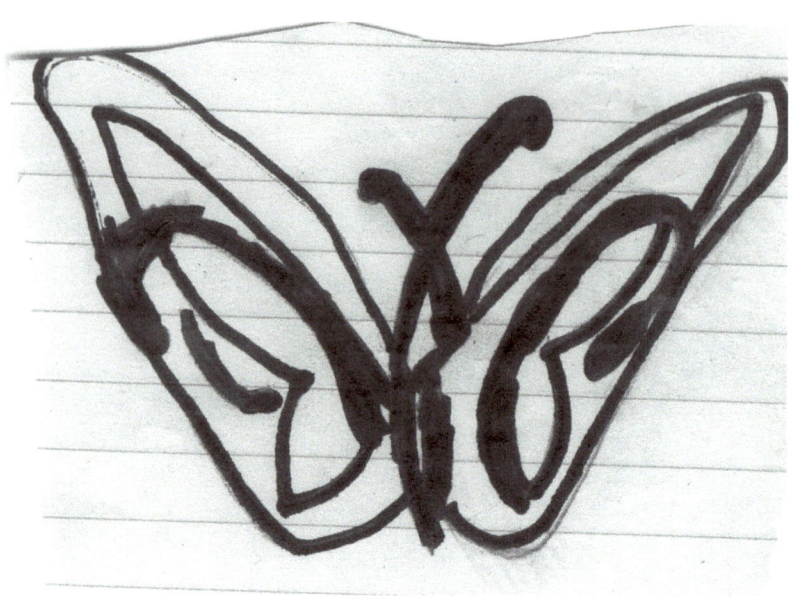

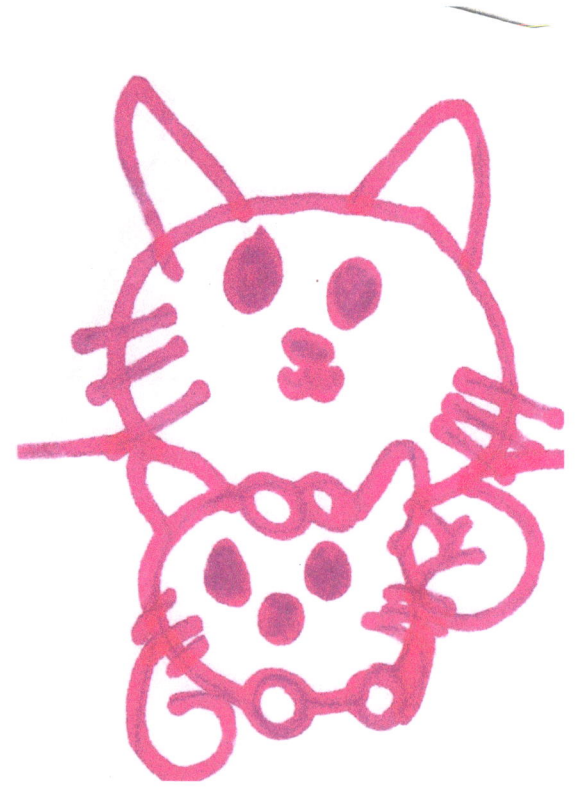

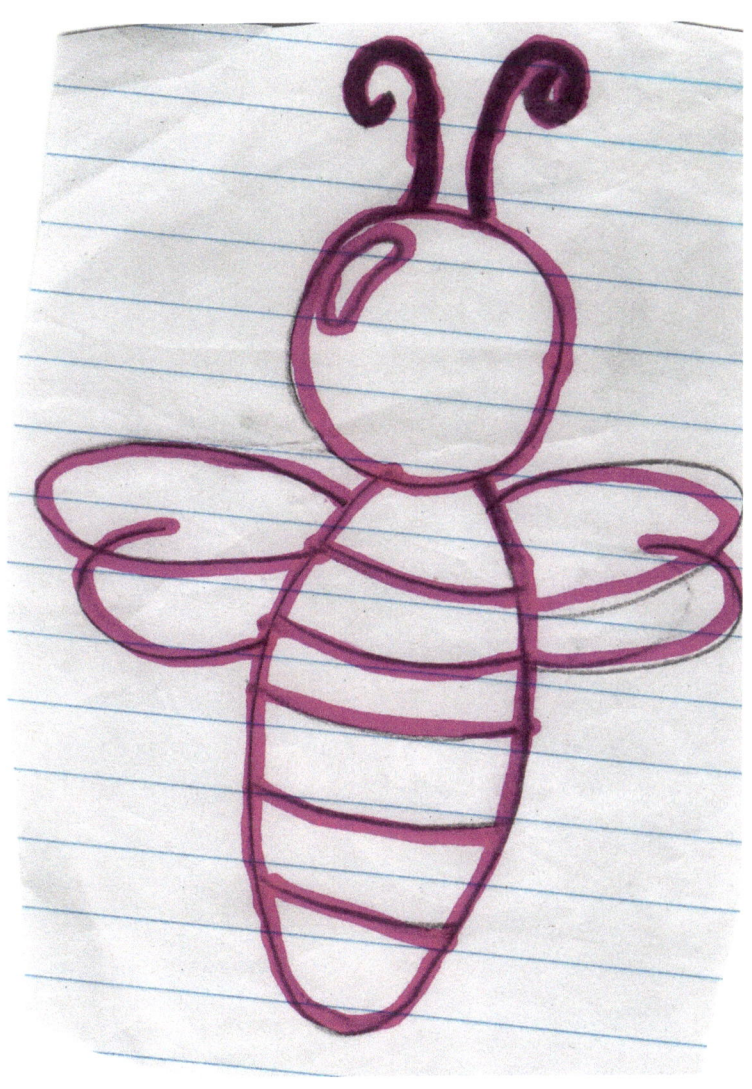

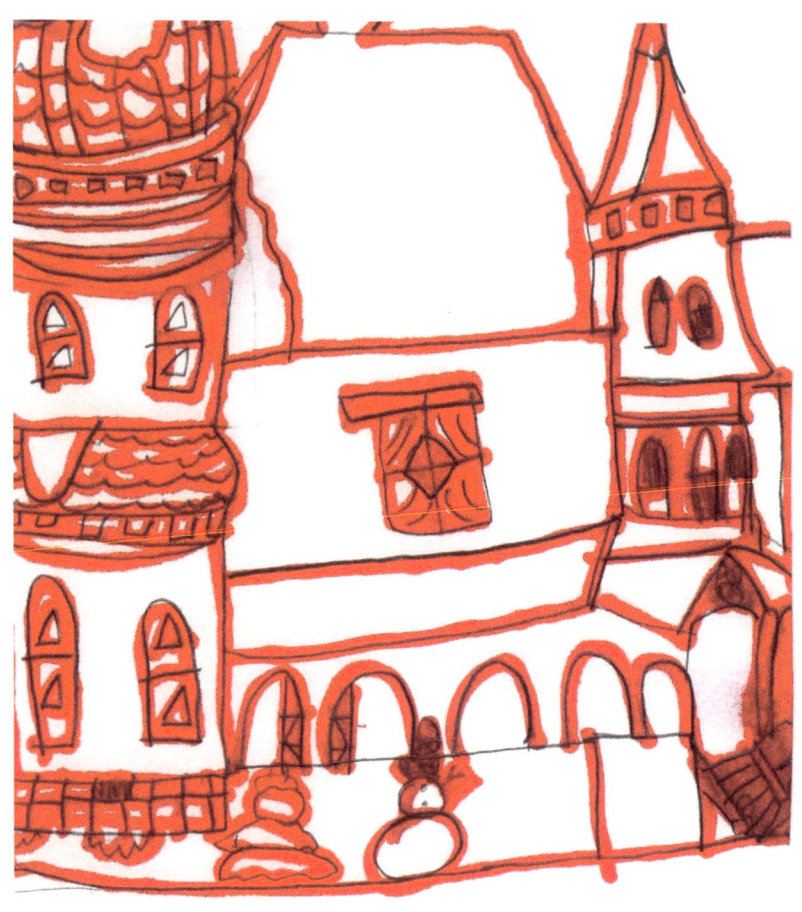

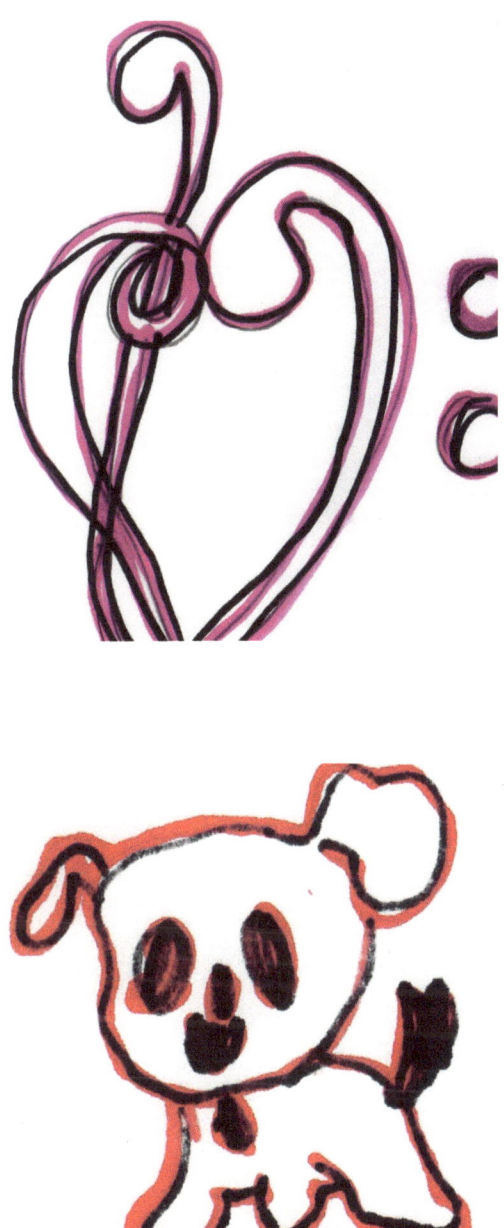

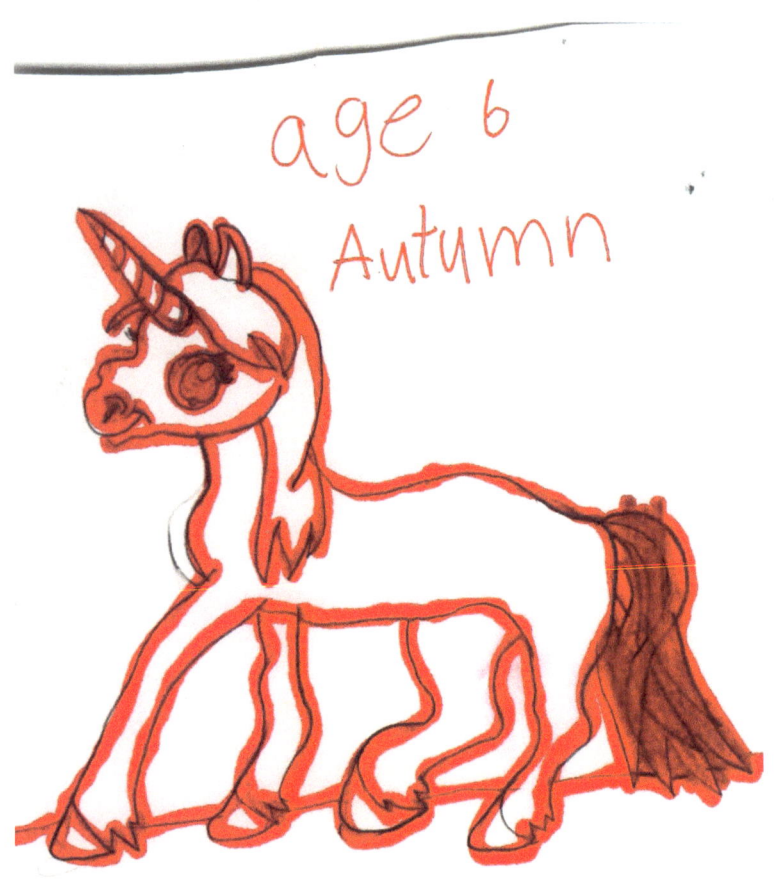

age 6
Autumn

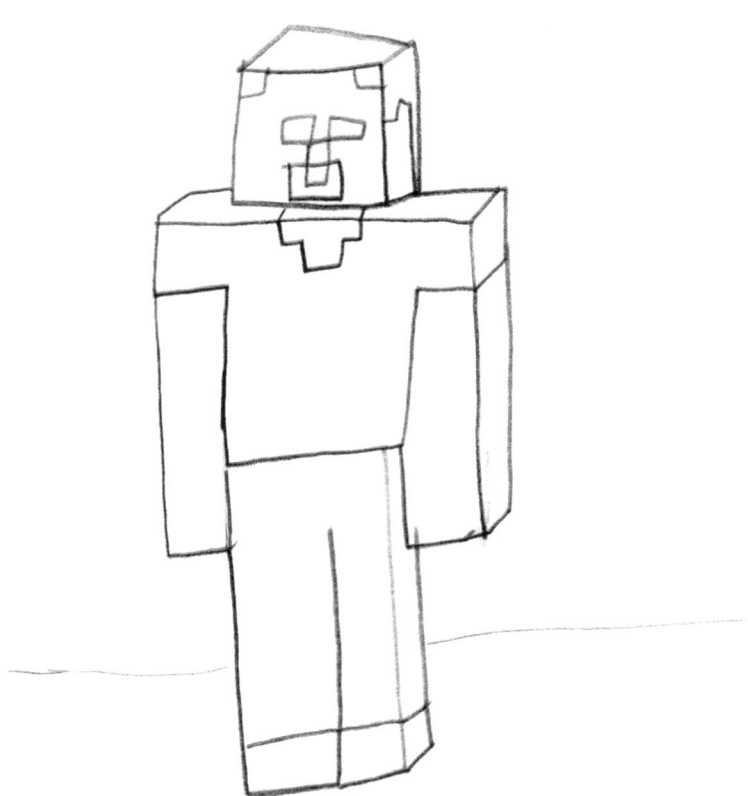

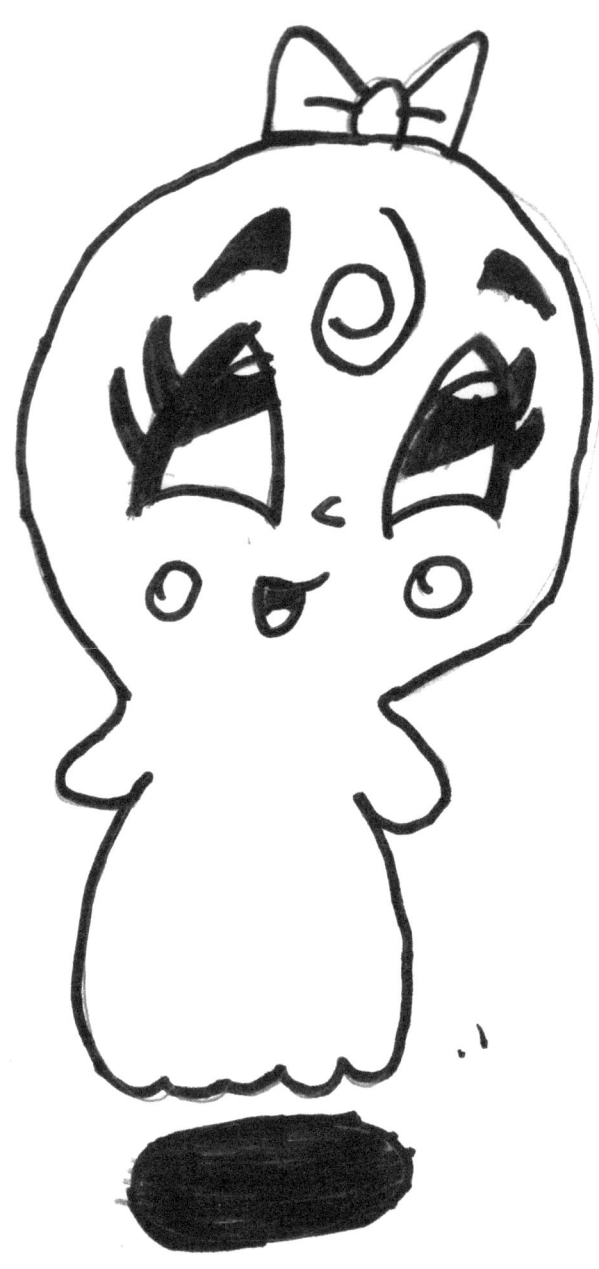

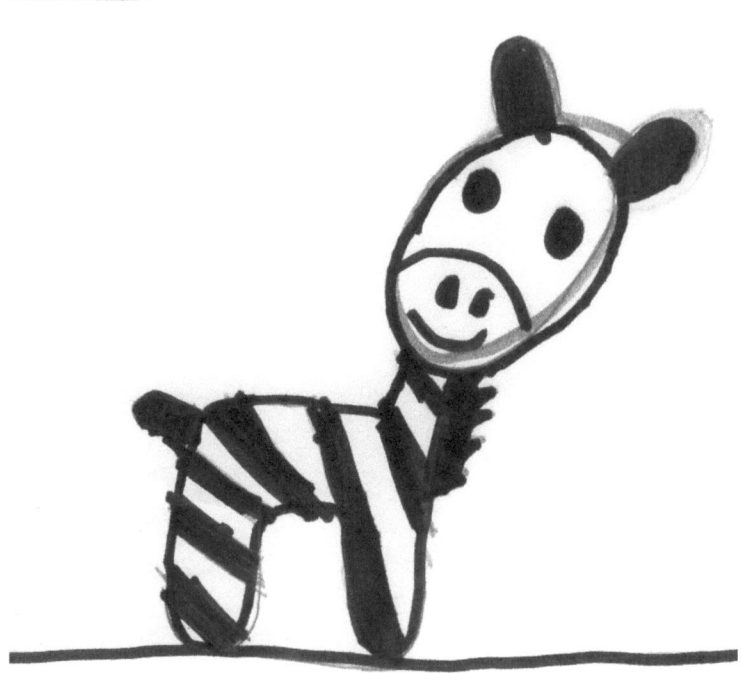

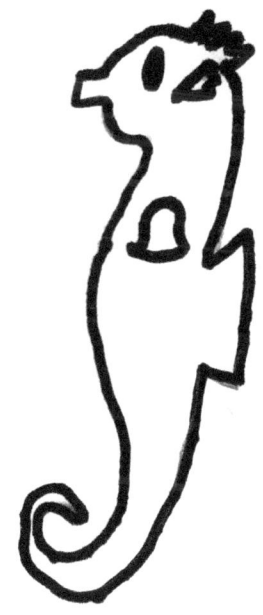

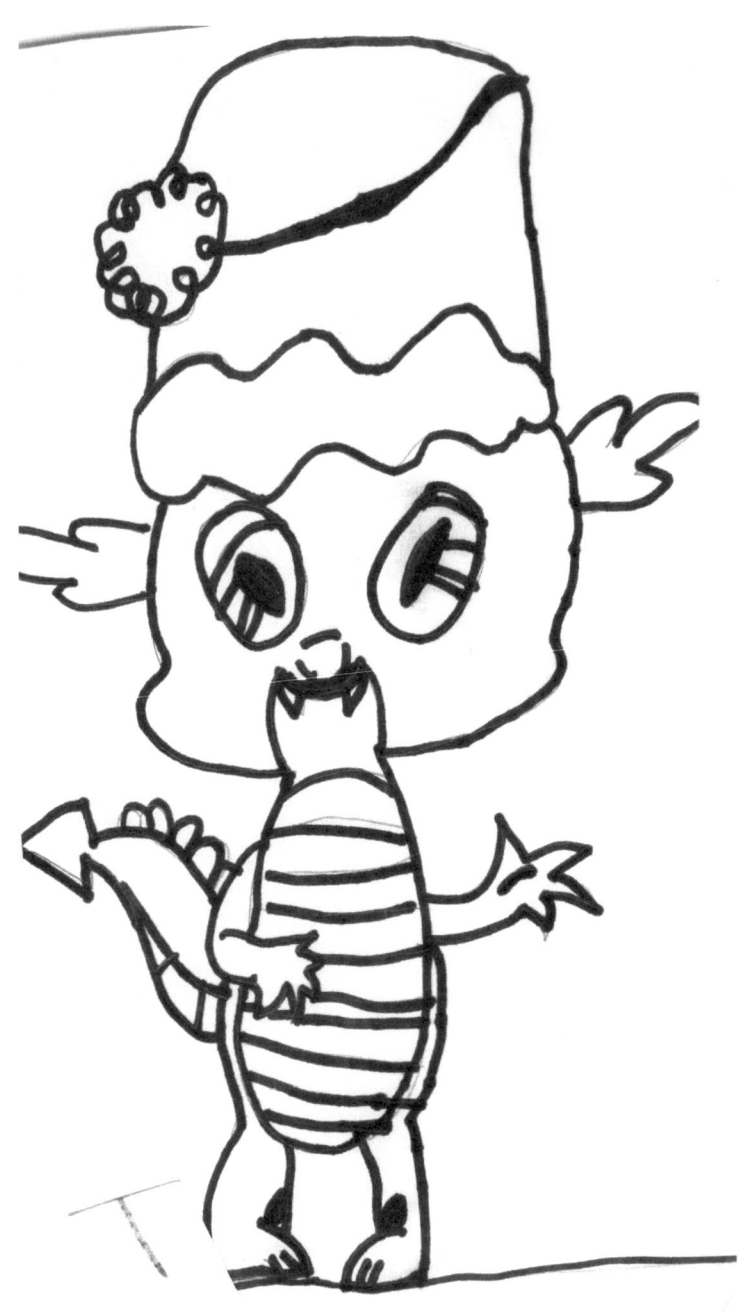

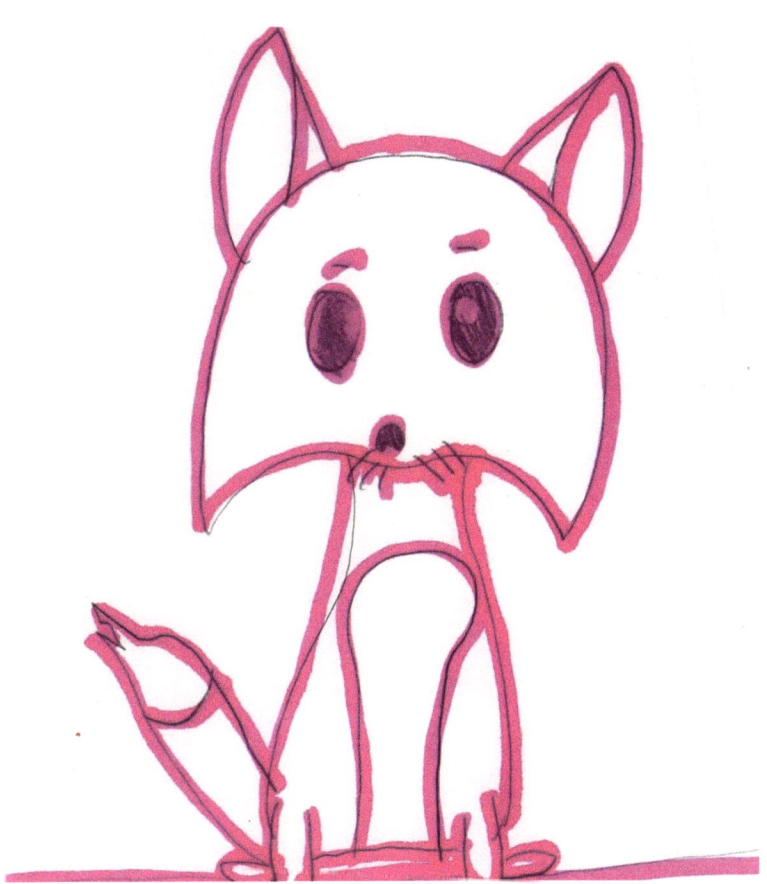

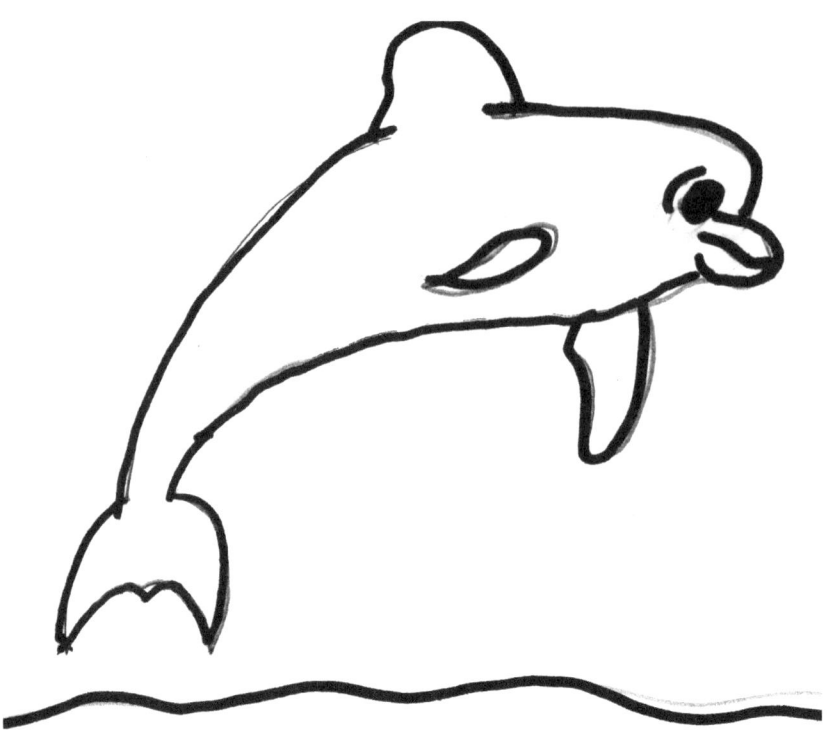

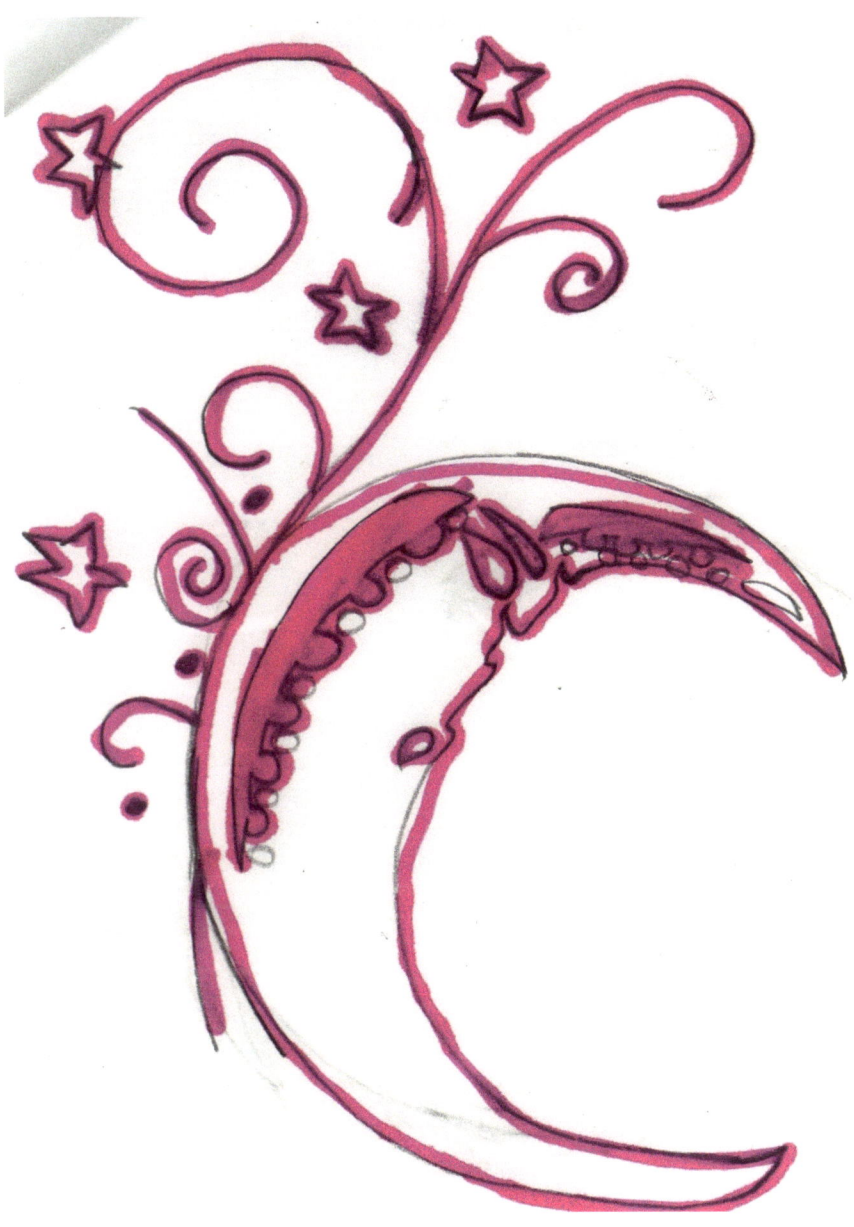

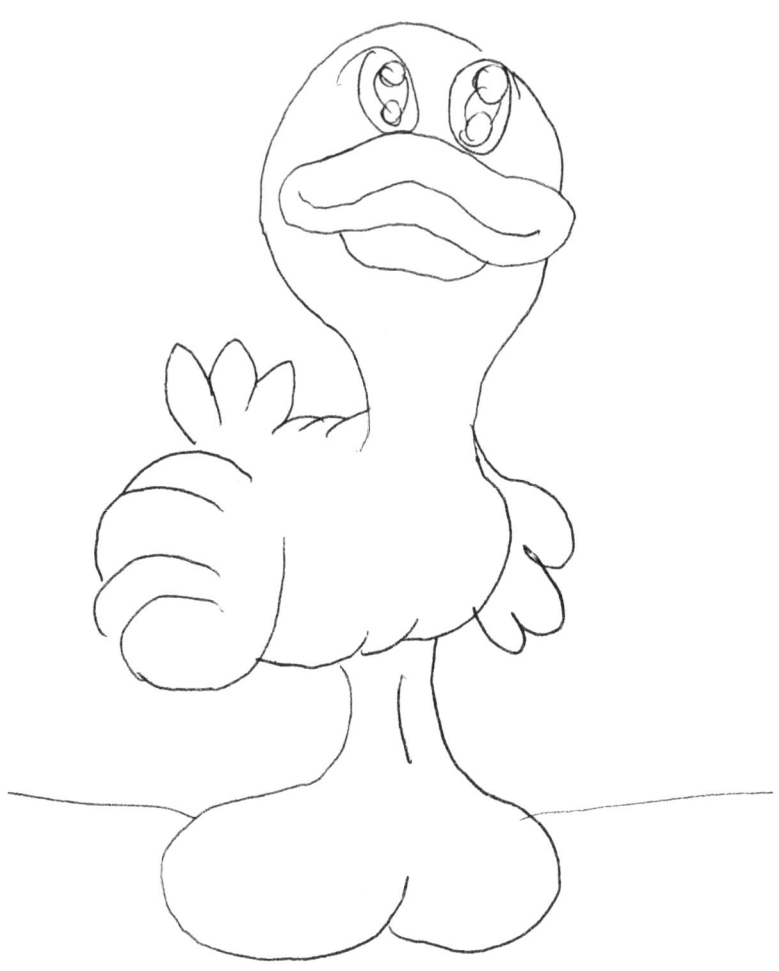

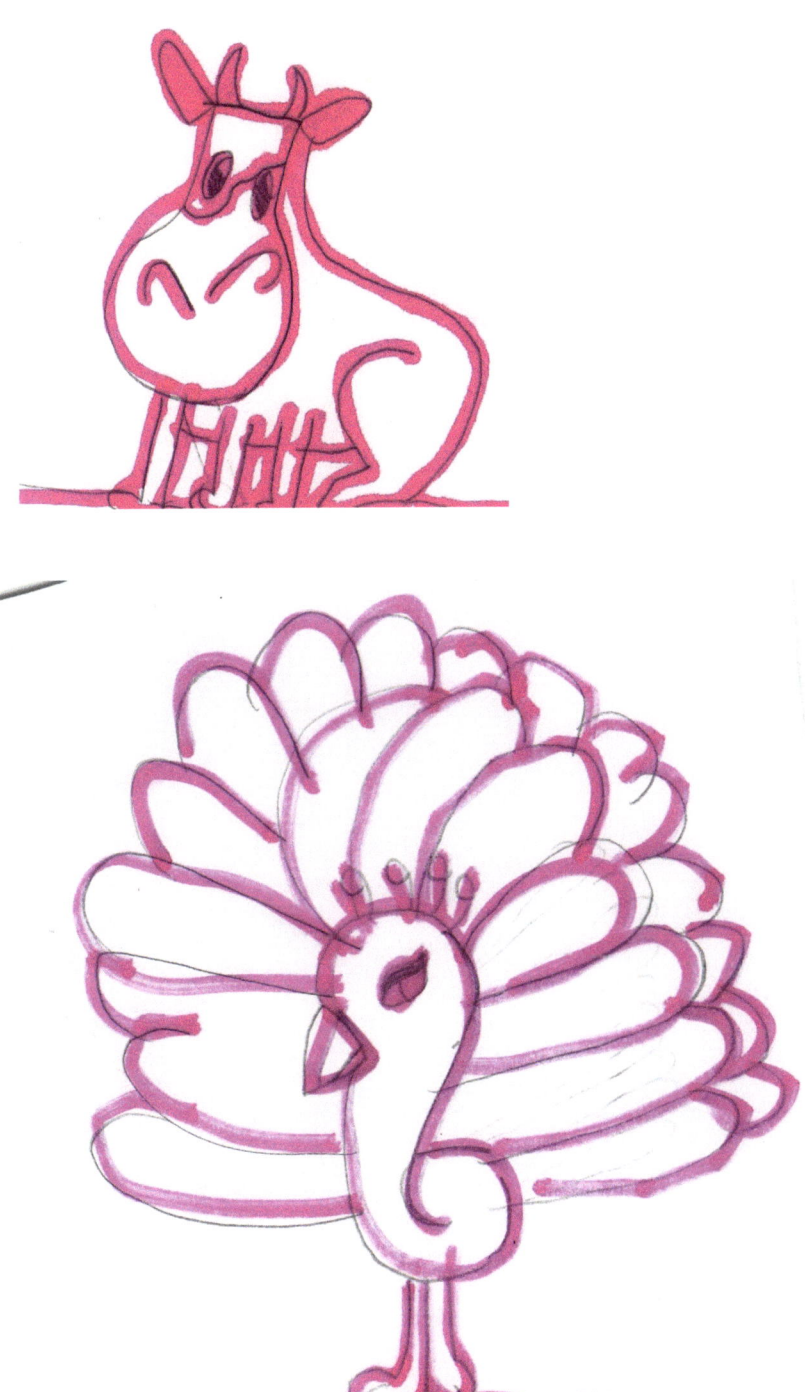

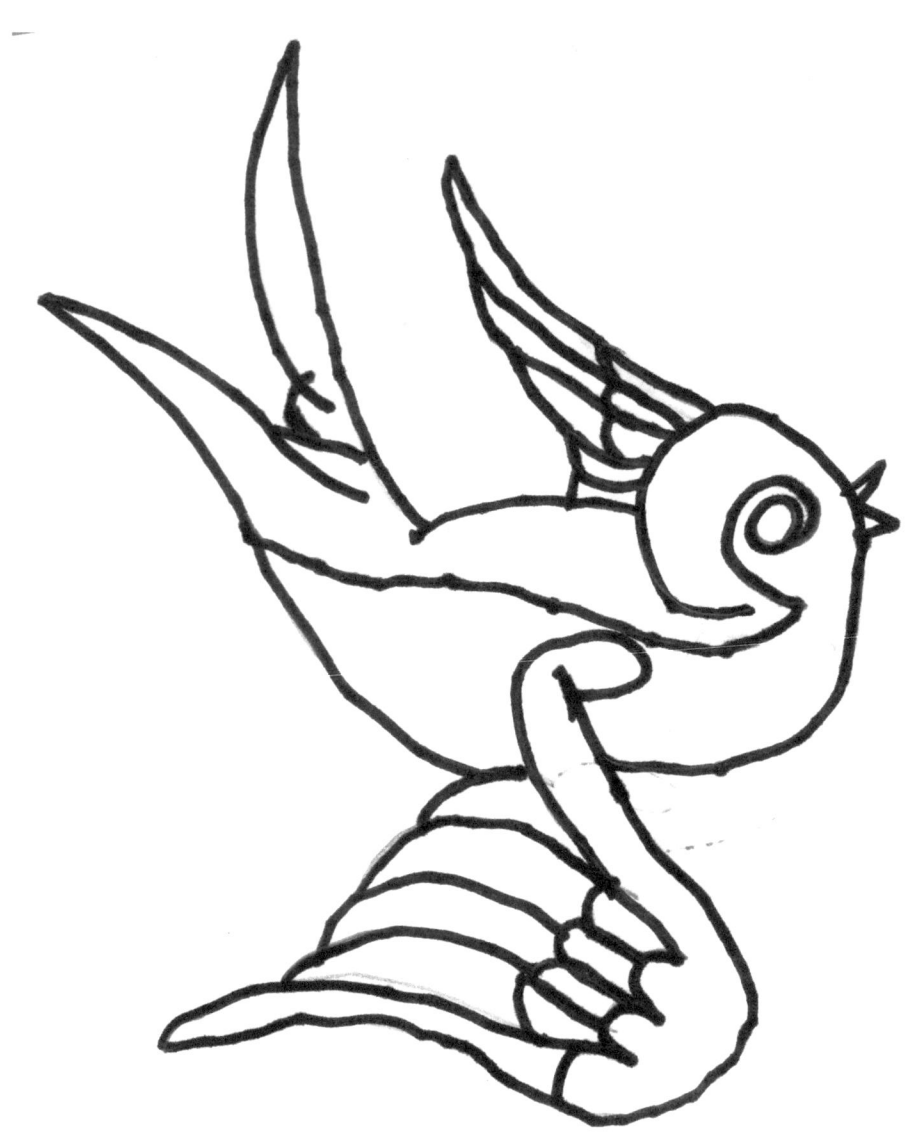

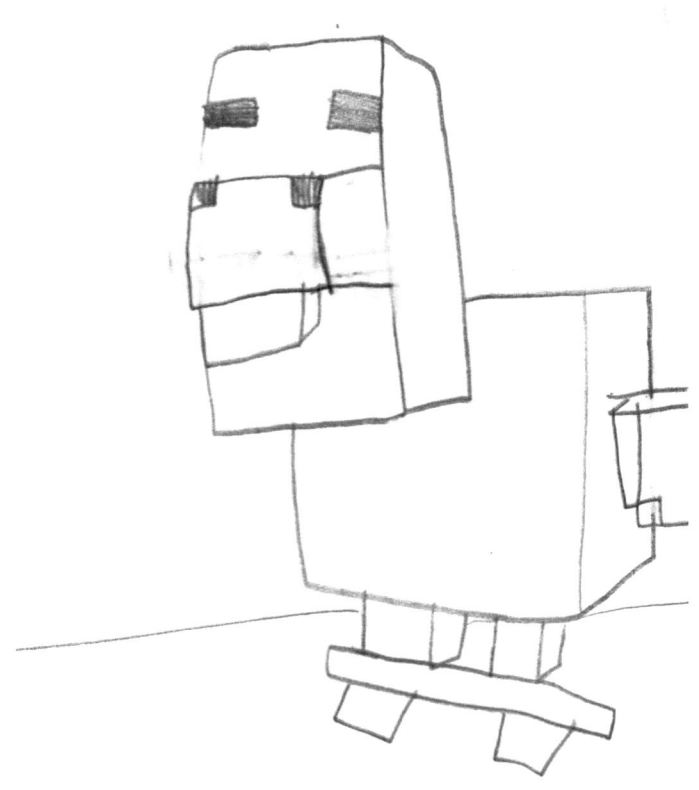

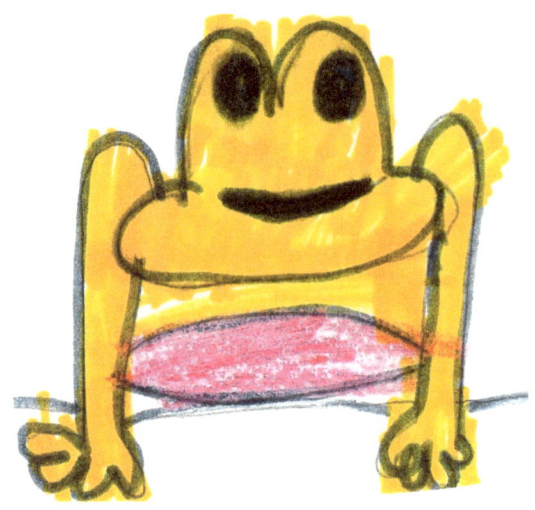

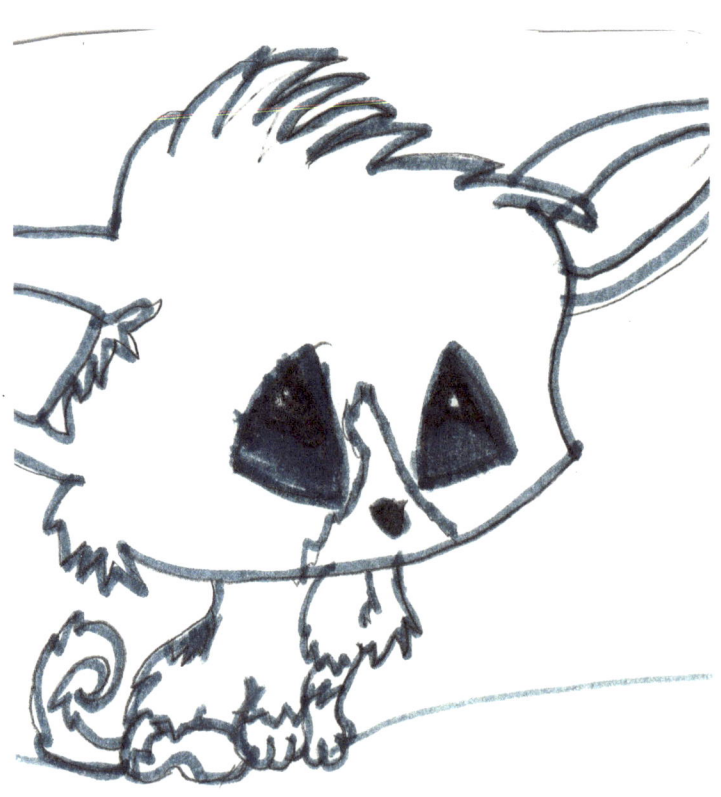

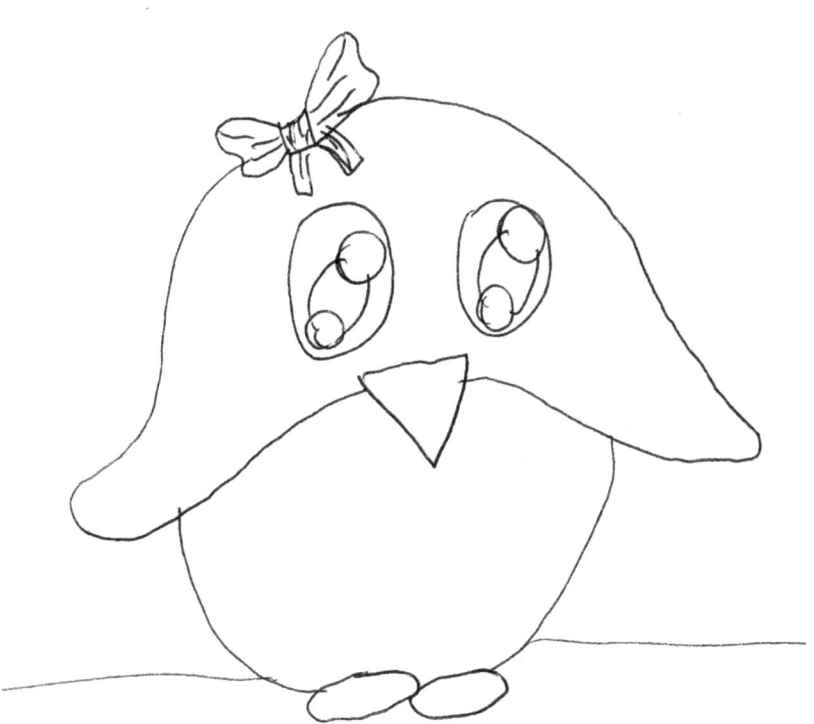

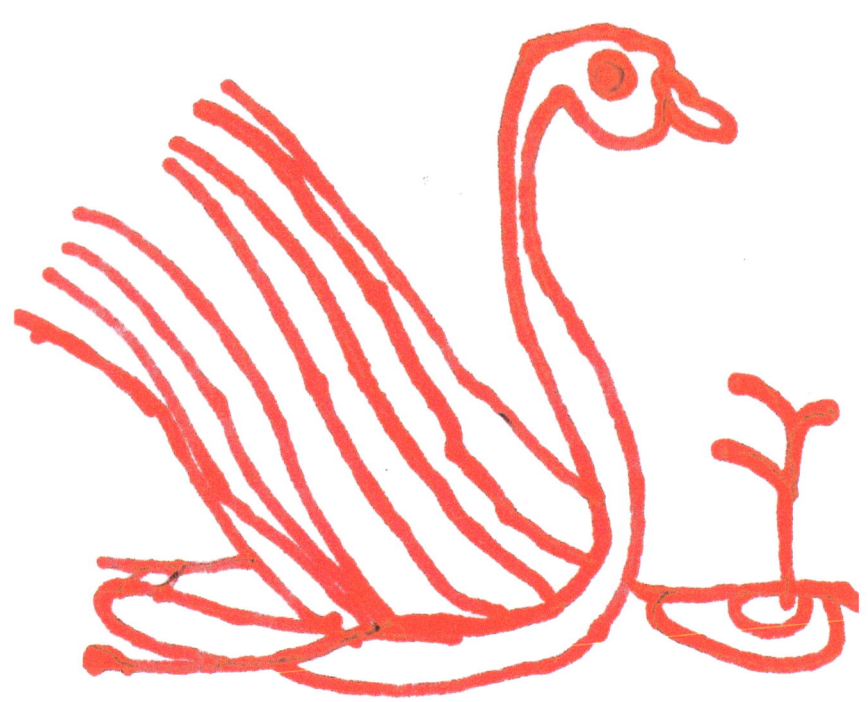

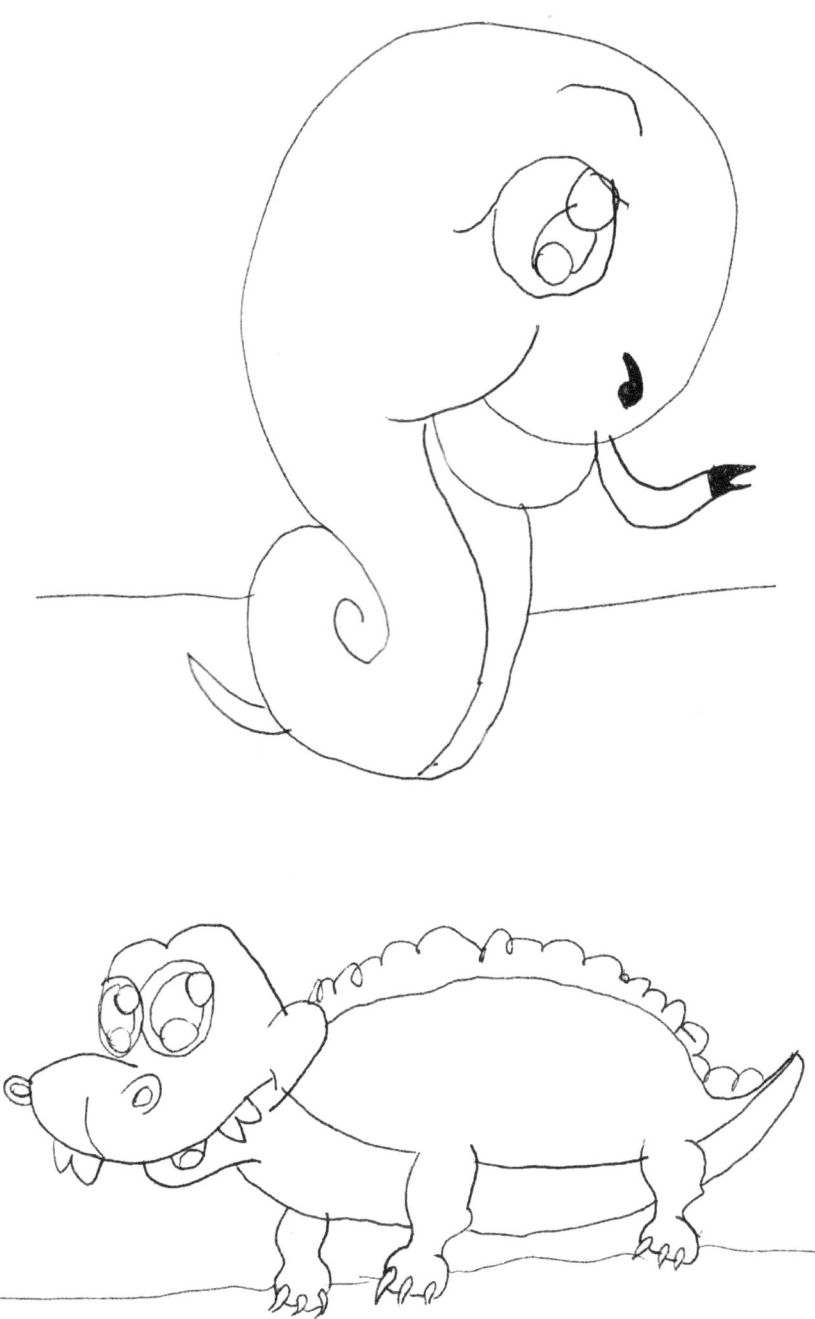

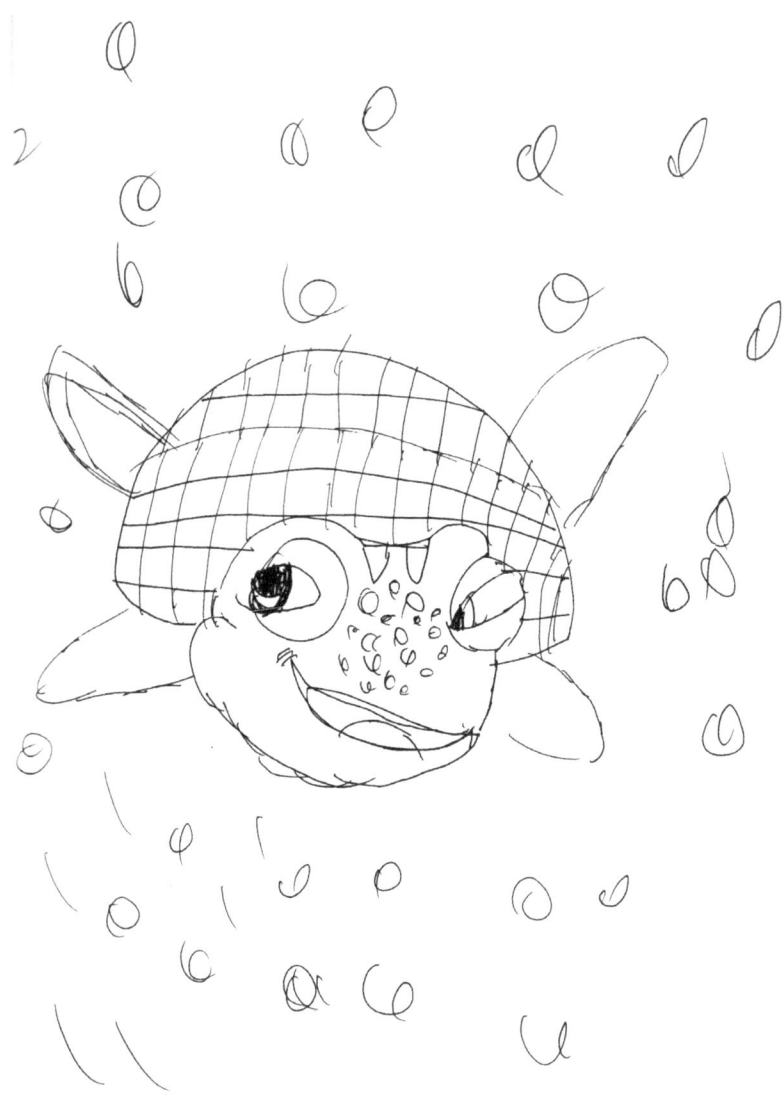

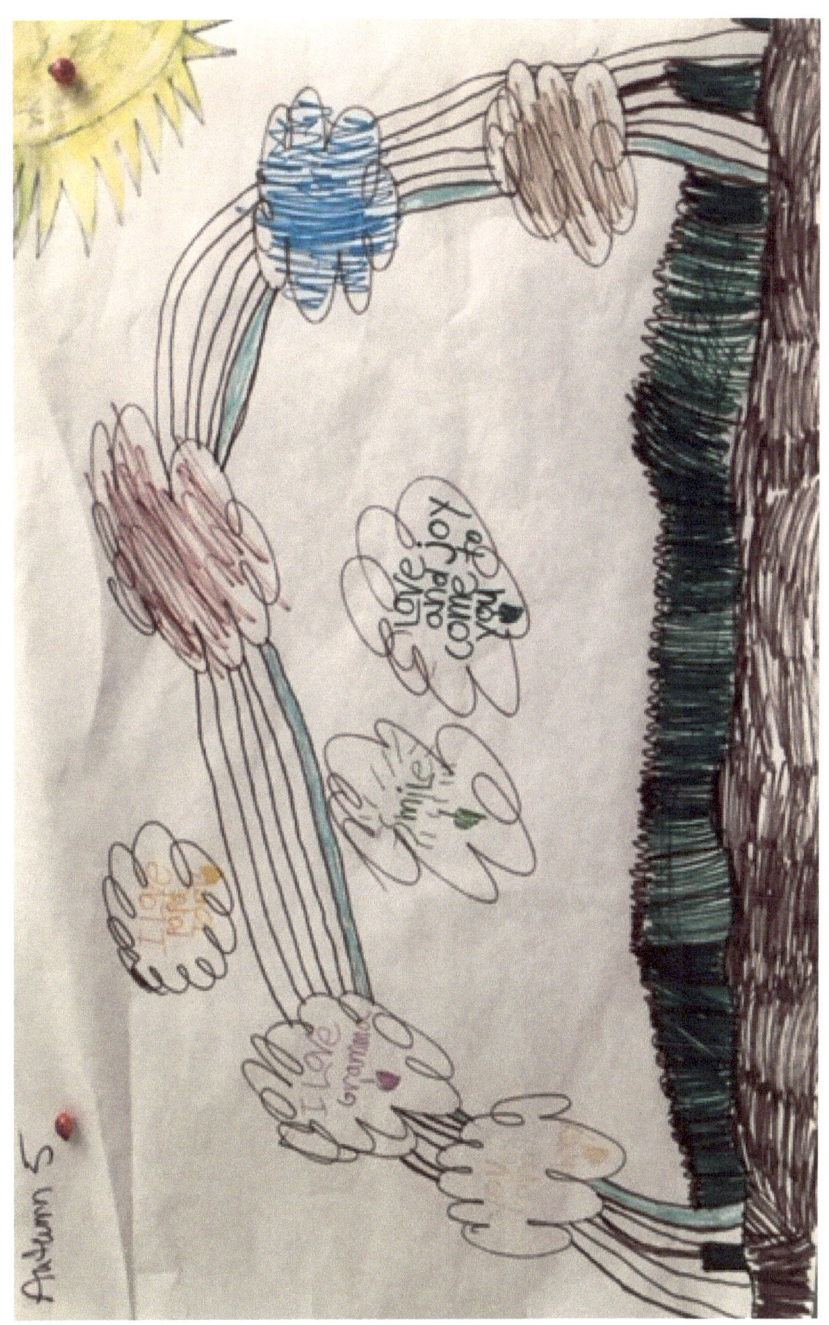

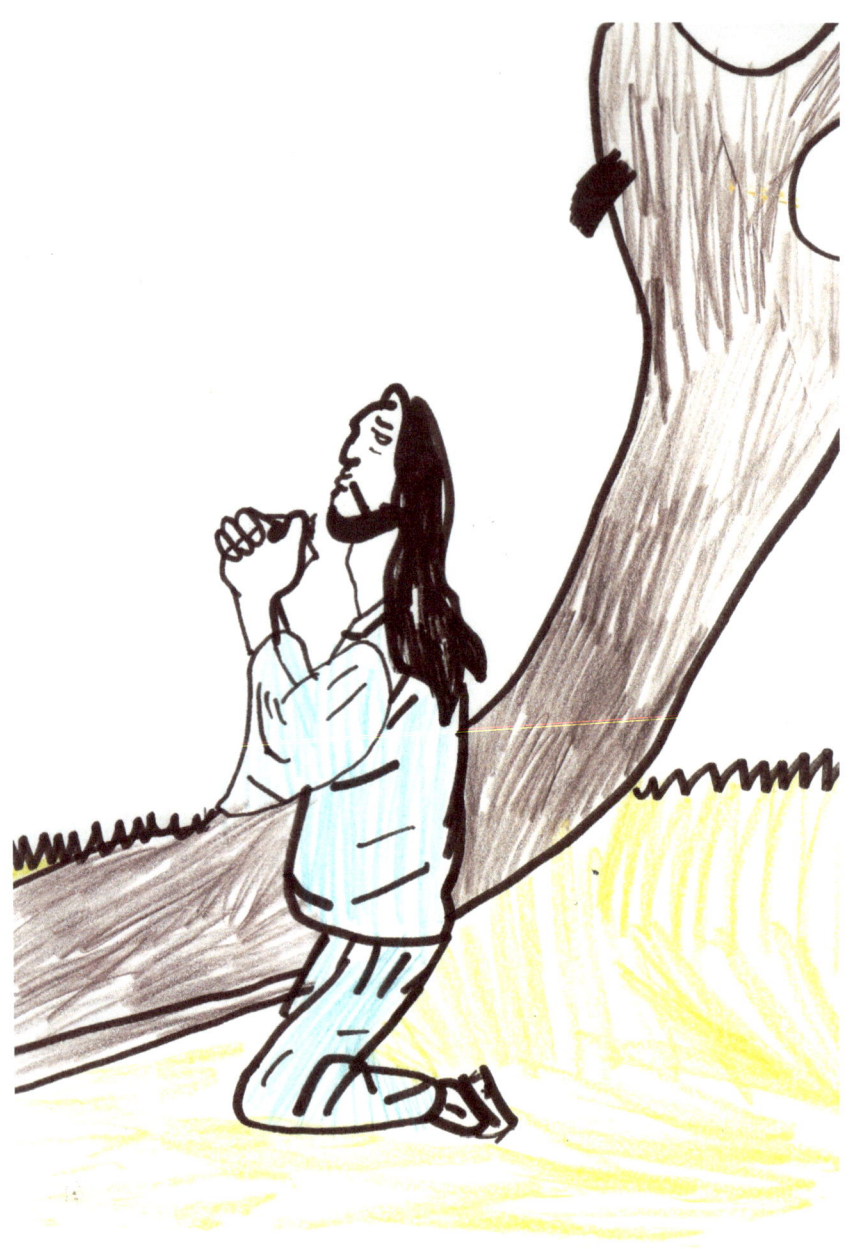

BUT JESUS SAID,
DON'T FORBID CHILDREN TO COME
UNTO ME: FOR SUCH IS THE
KINGDOM OF HEAVEN.

Luke 18:16

Make Me Smile

www.ingramcontent.com/pod-product-compliance
Lightning Source LLC
Chambersburg PA
CBHW040847180526
45159CB00001B/349